LIFE PALETTE
GOD MADE A MASTERPIECE...AND IT'S YOU!

DR. JEFFREY ALLEN LOVE

Tucson, AZ
in cooperation with 2911 publishing

Life Palette
Copyright © 2013 by Dr. Jeffrey Allen Love
All rights reserved. Published 2013
Dr. Jeffrey Allen Love serves as the lead/teaching pastor of Alive Church in Tucson, AZ. With success at an early age as a painter, art has always been a big part of his life. While pursuing art and music in college, Jeff felt compelled to go into church ministry and has served faithfully for over 25 years. He has a B.S. in Theology and a Doctorate in Ministry from PHX University of Theology.

All Bible quotations, unless otherwise indicated, are from the New Living Translation, copyright © 1996, 2004, 2007 by Tyndale House Foundation. Used by permission of Tyndale House Publishers Inc., Carol Stream, Illinois 60188. All rights reserved.

Other Bible versions used are:
New International Version, copyright © 1973, 1978, 1984, 2011 by Biblica, Inc. Used by permission. All rights reserved worldwide.
The Message, copyright © 1993, 1994, 1995, 1996, 2000, 2001, 2002. Used by permission of NavPress Publishing Group.

Adam Colwell's WriteWorks Publishing, in cooperation with 2911 publishing
Printed in the United States of America
www.lifepalette.com
Edited by Adam Colwell, Julianne Colwell, and Dave Ficere
Cover design by Deborah Cheves
Typesetting by Andrew MacKay
Printing by Arizona Lithographers, Laura Davis
All paintings by Dr. Jeffrey Allen Love
ISBN 978-0-9892057-3-3

What they're saying about
Life Palette

Someone once said, "The best the world can get is you, being you, with God all over you." My good friend, Dr. Jeffrey Allen Love, has taken this idea to a new level. In his new book *Life Palette*, he takes you on a journey of discovery of your God-created, God-designed life. God is the artist and you are the art. *Life Palette* helps you see yourself the way God sees you. As an artist, a musician, and a pastor, Jeff enlists his heart and art to help us rise above the human tendency of living big lives in small ways. *Life Palette* empowers you to open up your life and live expansively. After all, you are God's workmanship…and God don't make no junk!

Dr. Ed Delph
Nationstrategy, Phoenix, Arizona

For a couple of years, I've carried a piece of art canvas around in my wallet where I've written, "God wants to create a masterpiece on the canvas of my life." Not until reading Jeff's book was I able to recognize exactly what that meant or how it would transpire. Jeff Love has led me to discover what my unique life masterpiece looks like, and provided the tools and insight to begin to shape my life into the ultimate design. You'll find *Life Palette* beyond inspiring.

Steve Lacy
Founder and CEO, JSL Solutions and creator of
StreamingChurch.tv, ChurchApplive.com and MyFlock.com

In his book *Life Palette*, Jeff takes an imaginative approach to create an artistic metaphor of God's role as the painter of masterpieces: you and I. Jeff teaches us what qualities and characteristics are necessary on our color palettes, while at the same time giving us a greater understanding of how a painting is made into a masterpiece. This colorful and inspiring book will change the way you view your participation with God in shaping your life into a work of great beauty and light, or by working against Him to become a reflection of a lifeless forgery. Jeff's teaching approach is direct and simple, like a paint-by-number, yet with a depth requiring an intentional response on our part.

Julie Joiner
Editor

I teach principles of "Intentional Living" and my wife is an accomplished artist, so my interest was piqued when I saw Dr. Love's book *Life Palette*. The principles Dr. Love teaches speak to me, and I think they will speak to you as well. Our God is an intentional God, who intentionally loved us so much that He died for us. His intentionality is also proved in how He has gifted each of us to serve Him and one another as we live out our faith. Jeff is a regular contributor to my radio program, and I'm happy to recommend his book as I believe it will help you navigate your own faith journey.

Dr. Randy Carlson
President, Family Life Communications,
and Host of the "Intentional Living" radio program.

Picture a painter's studio, per chance a double car garage, in Tucson, Arizona. As you look around, you see all the accoutrements of a skilled painter. There stands the easel and alongside the easel a table and on the table lay the palette, and the varied colors of paints chosen for the day's work. Brushes and knives are there also.

Picture a pastor's study, large mahogany desk, and plush chair. Book shelves are standing from floor to ceiling, full of scholarly books on the Bible and theology, history, and apologetics. Undergraduate and graduate degrees line the wall.

These two work places seem worlds apart…and yet not so. Welcome to the studio and study of Dr. Jeffrey Allen Love. You will enter his life and thoughts through the pages of *Life Palette*. In this book, the paraphernalia from Dr. Love's studio become metaphorical. The eternal values found in his study come alive as artistic words are used to define them.

Alton B. Tomlin Ph.D.
Life Church, Fort Collins, Colorado

I grew up with an artist: my dad. Unfortunately, his artistic talents did not rub off on me! But it doesn't matter. Even though I'm not skilled at painting, I can appreciate and learn from others who are. Dr. Jeffrey Allen Love's *Life Palette* provides one of those opportunities.

Life Palette is interactive: it shows rather than merely tells. Jeff does a great job of drawing (no pun intended!) the reader into the vivid story of how God gifts each one with their very own, custom-designed, palette for living the life He has designed. You will benefit from reading this book, but you will benefit more by doing what's in this book.

Steve Tanner
Christian radio announcer and voiceover artist, Tucson, Arizona

As an artist, I can appreciate Jeff's ability to take his knowledge and experience in painting and use it as an analogy of our walk with God. The choices we make as artists impact our work just as the choices we make in life affect our relationship with God. Just like an artist needs to have a good understanding of what makes a good painting and how to apply it to a canvas, we need to have a good understanding of the Gospel and how to apply it to our lives. Jeff does a great job of showing how a sovereign God can create a masterpiece with our lives, if we will humble ourselves and seek His riches instead of our own.

Phil Starke
Award-winning painter and workshop teacher, Tucson, Arizona
(See Phil's "Between the Palette Scrapings" features throughout this book)

Dedication

This book is dedicated to my grandson Ender. Your life as God's masterpiece began just as I finished the last chapters of this book. Seeing your life begin reminded me of how God has created us all as His masterpiece. Karli (my daughter) and Theron (my son-in-law), you had a major part in creating Ender (you did good). I know you will be great parents in helping Ender live life as His masterpiece!

Acknowledgements

Thanks to my wife and comrade in arms, Kathy. You have always been my incredible support in everything I have done. You, of all people, have paid a tremendous price for this book to be written as you have willingly given the thing that matters most to you, my time. If I had the choice to take this journey in life with you again, I would.

To my four kids, Karli, Kadi, Kristi, and Joel. You all have helped me to see God's work as His masterpieces in real time. I am so glad that I'm your dad! You have taken my life to depths that I could not imagine without you in my life. If God lined up all the kids in the world and told me to pick any four kids to be mine, I would choose you.

To my sis, Julie. Thanks for your input as an editor and writer. You and Jim are a big support. Little sis, Roni Kay, as always, you keep me real.

To Mike, Sharon, Jason, and all my amazing staff at Alive Church. It is such an incredible privilege to do what we do together. You are always an encouragement both through your support and your willingness to challenge me to live my life as the masterpiece God created me to be. We've been through a lot together, many things I don't want to go through again. But I'm grateful I've gone through them with all of you—and that I would do again.

Alive Church, you are off the charts when it comes to a church. Your willingness to allow me to be creative, take chances, and to risk to live out our mission of "Leading people to Jesus, Training people to follow Jesus, and Sending people to lead for Jesus" is epic! I speak for all of the pastoral staff when I tell you that it is an honor to partner with you for the sake of eternity.

Adam Colwell, you are a man of incredible patience and persistence. You are truly an encourager. This project is complete because of your passionate pursuit and belief in me and the message of *Life Palette*. I appreciate all of your input, coaching, and grace for all of the deadlines that I missed!

Dr. T, thank you for sharing your passion for theology and teaching the Word. Your guidance in these areas has been invaluable to me over the years, especially your willingness to help me navigate the application of a creative idea like *Life Palette* to theological concepts. I'm grateful that you are my stepfather. You and mom are an incredible blessing not only to me, but to the many lives God has used the two of you to minister to throughout your years of pastoring. Love you, mom. You have always been so supporting and encouraging. You're my favorite mom. Thank you for leading me to follow Jesus.

I want to especially thank Mike Gray for all his help with social media, and to his team in creating the web presence for *Life Palette*. If anyone has ever been given the spiritual gift of connecting the dots, it's you!

There are many who have made an impact in my life to take the path I've taken to ultimately help me shape my Life Palette. Dad, grandparents, and the many mentors I've had the privilege of having throughout my life, I am so grateful for how each of you allowed God to work in and through you. I'm especially blessed to have been influenced by a few great men who were my pastors. I will do my best to pass on to others the incredible gift you have given me.

Jesus, thank you for allowing me to experience your amazing love and grace. My view of life was total hopelessness before I met you. Knowing that you have created me as your masterpiece is beyond anything I can imagine. Here it is, my life is yours to do with what you wish, and I trust you as the artist of my life.

Contents

Chapter 1 – You Are a Masterpiece 1

Chapter 2 – Values, Values, Values. 13

Chapter 3 – A Valuable Example. 29

Chapter 4 – Through Squinted Eyes 43

Chapter 5 – Good, Bad or U-g-l-y. 59

Chapter 6 – Color Harmony. 77

Chapter 7 – Creativity. 91

Chapter 8 – Consistency 105

Chapter 9 – Keeping a Limited Palette 119

Chapter 10 – The Importance of Scraping. 131

Chapter 11 – Chasing the Light 143

Chapter 12 – The Finishing Touches 155

*Each chapter concludes with applicable Palette Points
perfect for your individual study or small group study.*

Chapter One

You Are a Masterpiece

You are a masterpiece.

How do I know? Because God says so. "For we are God's masterpiece. He has created us anew in Christ Jesus, so we can do the good things he planned for us long ago." (Ephesians 2:10) You may not feel like it at the moment. You may look at your life and see yourself as someone whose life is out of balance, headed in the wrong direction, or even a complete failure. Or perhaps you have a sense of agreement with being a masterpiece, not so much because you truly believe it, but because you know it's the right thing to believe. Perhaps you're like Stuart Smalley, the Saturday Night Live character, looking in the mirror and trying to convince yourself, "I'm good enough, I'm smart enough and, doggone it, people like me!" Wherever you are, it's tiring trying to recognize your own priceless value when you don't feel it inside or see it in how you live your life.

There is a better way!

Our family loves to spend time vacationing in Durango, Colorado especially because it's a great artistic community. One day, in one of the town's galleries, the work of a particular artist grabbed our attention. As we stood admiring his work, the gallery director began to share with us a little of his story—and she made a statement about the artist that has changed my life. Having been an artist myself since my youth, the thought was not new to me, but this time it was an "A-ha!" moment.

She said this: "He has really developed his palette."

Suddenly, the statement was no longer about the artist or the artwork. It was about life. I began processing the words in my mind, and couldn't wait to get back to the computer to start writing a teaching series based on those words.

The palette is an essential tool for an artist because it's where they mix the colors that they dip their brush into to paint their masterpiece. The colors on the palette are very personal and unique for the masterpiece the artist has in mind. Most important, the colors that appear on the canvas can only be mixed from what's on the palette. In other words, the painting will never rise above the quality of paint on the palette.

> **How you develop your Life Palette will cause those around you to take notice.**

I was recently painting in beautiful Yellowstone National Park and realized the limitations of the palette I'd developed as an artist. Living in the desert southwest, I don't normally paint the incredibly vibrant greens that I found in Yellowstone; the greens in the desert are much duller, eliminating the need for a bright yellow on my palette. Until I found an art store, I simply couldn't capture the greens of Yellowstone. My palette was limiting me. The colors on an artist's palette will vary based on style and the desired end result, but make no mistake; what's on the palette either limits or empowers the artist as they paint. I have since painted several times in Yellowstone and love to paint from my Yellowstone references. I continue to master the beautiful greens as seen in "Up To The Rivers Edge" in this book.

That day in Durango, the difference between that artist and every other one in that gallery wasn't that his natural God-given gift was greater than the others. It wasn't that the subject matter of his paintings—western art and landscapes—was something uniquely unusual.

What set this artist apart from the rest of the gallery was how he had developed his palette.

Your *Life* Palette

What is it that makes some people a success or not a success at something? It's not always the most talented, whether in business, sports, medicine, ministry, or any number of career choices. Nor is it those who just happened to get lucky, or are at the right place at the right time. So what is it? What makes the difference?

It's this. Each of us is given a palette in life. We make the choices that will develop our Life Palette. From this palette the color and composition of the *life you live* is determined. How you develop your Life Palette will cause those around you to take notice, pause, and consider the beauty of a life lived with direction and destiny compared to one lived aimlessly and without effect.

Perhaps you've heard it said that in life you are either in a crisis, just getting out of a crisis, or headed toward one. That is by no means a doom and gloom statement. It's just the way life is. Most of what happens to you is, unfortunately, out of your control. Yet one thing you can control is how your Life Palette is developed. And your success or failure will be a direct result of that Life Palette.

Why does someone face circumstances that seem insurmountable and become a better person through them, even leveraging them to their benefit and the benefit of those around them? They've developed their Life Palette. They may not intentionally know they've done it, but they have. And in this book, you will discover how to develop your Life Palette—and allow God to paint your life as the masterpiece He designed you to be.

You can do what you wish with your life. You have been given the privilege by your Creator to completely mess up your life and make it a disingenuous forgery of what it could be, or you can do your part to become the masterpiece God created you to be. The palette He has to work with is up to you.

Life Palette

The Maker of the Masterpiece

If I asked you to describe a masterpiece painting, the first one likely to come to mind is Leonardo da Vinci's Mona Lisa. Hanging in the Louvre behind bulletproof glass in a controlled environment to preserve the pigment and the canvas, the Mona Lisa is well protected.

What makes the Mona Lisa a masterpiece? It's certainly not the subject matter. There have been millions of portraits of beautiful women painted throughout the centuries that would never be considered masterpieces. Did da Vinci have some secret paint or brushes no other artists knew existed? Actually, the material available to every art student today is much more advanced than what was available to da Vinci and his peers. The Mona Lisa is a masterpiece because of da Vinci's extraordinary skill and intellect.

With that in mind, it may be hard to describe yourself as a masterpiece. It somehow feels vain, arrogant, and even haughty to look at yourself that way. Maybe the opposite of self-pride is the problem. You don't believe you're beautiful enough on the inside to possibly be considered a work of art. You know who you are and what you've done. You know the ugliness of it, to the point that it even defines you.

But here's the key. It's not about your extraordinary skill, intellect, or lack of both. Nothing can change the fact that you're *already* created as a masterpiece. Nothing you think or do can undo that truth. Why? You're not the creator of the masterpiece to begin with. You're not the artist.

God is.

You are a masterpiece—not because you're a da Vinci who has painted every brush stroke of your life perfectly, or because every choice you've made was the right color for your life's canvas. You are a masterpiece—not because you stood before your life's canvas at a young age and created a perfect composition that would fulfill your every dream, hope and wish.

You are a masterpiece because God, as the *artist*, created you as His masterpiece.

While you're not the artist of your masterpiece, you have a role in becoming the masterpiece God created you to be. ***Your responsibility is to create the Life Palette*** for God, the master artist, to paint the canvas of your life every day with His beauty, love, and destiny. God is the artist who dips His brush into your thoughts, decisions, and actions. He is the one who creates the composition, mixing the colors on your palette, each brush stroke placed perfectly and intently. Your job is to make and protect the palette for God to work with.

To create your Life Palette, you need to discover:

- The things currently on your Life Palette keeping you from being the masterpiece God created you to be.

- The right life choices to mix on your Life Palette that will allow God to paint the canvas of your life as the true masterpiece He designed you to be.

- The values necessary for a healthy foundation to build the rest of your Life Palette upon, so regardless of what life brings your way, you can continue to live as a masterpiece.

- The character, relational skills, creativity, consistency, priorities, and attitudes needed for God to dip His brush into and paint your life.

- The importance of keeping your Life Palette clean and fresh with the knowledge and abilities that will perpetuate a life lived as a masterpiece with an ever-increasing value.

Sadly, it's easy to create a Life Palette that's bad; one that will lead to your life being lived as a forgery rather than a masterpiece. It's a lot like growing weeds; it doesn't take talent or discipline, it only requires neglect. One of my earliest jobs as a kid was going out into the fields of my grandfather's farm to remove the unwanted weeds invading the crops. My grandfather kept his fields clean because he understood weeds affected the end result of his harvest. I remember driving by neighboring farmers' fields full of weeds and how grandpa always commented how the fields were a reflection of the farmer. Anyone can grow weeds, and anyone can create a bad Life Palette that'll result in living far worse than the masterpiece life God designed for you.

Between the Palette Scrapings with Phil Starke

Primary colors are the foundation for color. Every other color is a modifier; they are all peripheral. Too many colors on a palette will make things muddy.

Cleaning up your Life Palette

As an artist cleans his palette, he's left with palette scrapings—the leftover mixed paint that becomes gray and is no longer useable where pure color is needed. You may feel there are similar colorless scrapings in your life, choices that have caused you pain and led you so far off track that you feel your future has no destiny.

Know there is hope! You can clean your Life Palette and start over. It is possible. God is the God of new opportunities. In Isaiah 43:19 He says this: "For I am about to do something new. See, I have already begun! Do you not see it?" As long as you have a pulse, He has a destiny for your life—and that destiny will always include you becoming His masterpiece. It is never too late!

Three attitude checks will position you to clean and begin preparing your Life Palette:

1. Don't blame God. When you look at the canvas of your life and are not satisfied with the results, it's easy to blame God by falsely believing He made you with certain character flaws or weaknesses that have resulted in your life looking like a forgery rather than a masterpiece. You can easily continue to blindly hope something will change.

The attitude of blame is something you must clean off of your Life Palette. You may say, "But you don't know my life story." And you're right, I don't—and I don't need to. This is about knowing and understanding God as your loving Heavenly Father, as the artist who proclaims you to be His masterpiece. When you blame Him for things in your life, you're simply saying to Him that He's not doing a good job as the artist and that you, frankly, could do better. Yet the truth is He's willing to do whatever is necessary for you to live as His masterpiece. Paul tells you, "God showed his great love for us by sending Christ to die for us while we were still sinners." (Romans 5:8) It's not His fault. You determine what He has to work with on your Life Palette.

> **Nothing can change the fact that you're already created as a masterpiece.**

2. Don't worry about what others think. Who decides what constitutes a masterpiece? Vincent Van Gogh once said, "Painting is a faith, and it imposes the duty to disregard public opinion." He understood the public can be too subjective; too influenced by their self-centered passions. In the same way, others in your life—your parents, friends or bosses—can't decide what'll make you a masterpiece. The only one truly qualified to decide if a work of art is a masterpiece is the one who painted it, the artist: the person who studied art, worked on their craft and talent, and has truly developed their palette to see when a painting needs improvement, or when it is ready to display.

3. Trust that God knows what He's doing as the artist. God, and no one else, knows how to make your life into the masterpiece He created you to be. Remember Ephesians 2:10. You can trust God to make you into exactly what He's destined you to be as you do your part of aligning your Life Palette with what He, as the artist, determines will make you a masterpiece. Like a novice artist wants to know the successful artist's secrets, tricks, and even favorite tube of color, you must be willing to learn and develop the discipline, technique, and understanding required to develop your Life Palette.

Life Palette

Destined for success

In their article "Stringed Victory," Richard Jerome and Elizabeth McNeil told the story of Joshua Bell, a child prodigy on the violin who was a world-class musician by the young age of 29. Joshua always endeavored to be his best—at computers, chess, even video games. He pushed himself to succeed. One day, while visiting his hometown of Bloomington, Indiana, a small boy approached him. "You're Joshua Bell," he exclaimed. "You're famous!" Joshua humbly responded, "Well … not really." But the boy was insistent. "Yes, really … your name is on every video game in the arcade as the highest scorer!"

Different people define success in different ways. To create your Life Palette, you need a genuine definition for your success, and here's the formula to remember:

**Success =
Living *daily* as the masterpiece God created you to be**

Without a properly developed Life Palette, you cannot know true success in life. Your passions, desires, ambitions, and goals must all be aligned with creating a Life Palette that will help, and not hinder, you in achieving the destiny God has for you.

In the Bible, the psalmist wrote about those who "delight in the law of the Lord, meditating on it day and night. They are like trees planted along the riverbank, bearing fruit each season. Their leaves never wither, and they prosper in all they do." (Psalm 1:2-3) This verse provides a picture of what God desires for you as His masterpiece. His plan is that your life will always produce something of worth and value. His plan is that your life is lived like a tree with leaves that always bloom and give life, never dying away. His plan is that you will prosper in everything that you do. This prosperity is not a guarantee of health, wealth, and happiness, but it is an assurance that what God has in store for you is good and fulfilling. It is like the "rich and satisfying life" that Jesus said He came to give you in John 10:10. It's the kind of life that will give you more vigor and enthusiasm each day.

What is the condition for having this kind of prosperous life? The psalmist makes it clear: doing everything the Lord wants, achieved by constantly keeping in mind the directives of His Word. As you do this, you'll be freed from living your life according to what pleases others; instead, you will think, feel, and act according to what pleases God. You'll fill your Life Palette with the exact things the master artist needs.

It becomes automatic

I'll never forget when I first learned to drive. Before I turned 16, I bought a 1952 Volkswagen Beetle with a standard four speed transmission; it had a stick shift. It stayed parked in front of our family home until I got my driver's license. It wasn't much of a car: it had five different colors peeling through the previous paint jobs; the heater only worked in the summer, a distinct problem during Colorado winters; and the starter didn't work, which meant I had to push start it everywhere I went. No wonder I paid a whopping $200 for it, but it was my car!

As a beginner driver I could only do so much. My biggest challenge was learning to let out the clutch, give it just enough gas, and turn the steering wheel just right while trying to watch oncoming traffic and shift gears—all at the same time. I grew up in a small farming community in Ohio, so the big city traffic was terrifying to me. I thought I'd never get it; that driving would always be a lot of work. Then came that glorious day on my way home from school when, without realizing it, I shifted from first to second gear while turning into our neighborhood. I was no longer learning the technique; I was actually driving intuitively! I began to experience the joy of driving and having my independence. Traffic no longer made me nervous. I quit worrying about stalling the engine at a red light. Sometime in those brief months after getting my license, using the clutch, shifting, and navigating traffic became innate. Driving a standard transmission had become, well, automatic.

Developing your Life Palette will become automatic for you as well. If I asked you to list those whose lives you admire and that you believe represent God's masterpiece, you'd name people like Mother Teresa, the Rev. Billy Graham, President Abraham Lincoln or perhaps

Dr. Martin Luther King Jr. You might also list those who've impacted your life, but are unknown to others. Perhaps it's a business person who succeeded in your line of work, or a great teacher who influenced your life either in the classroom or in their ability to make a difference in the lives of their students. Some would list a clergyman, a coach, a parent, or perhaps a sibling.

> **God's destiny for your life will always include you becoming His masterpiece.**

Yet regardless of how you arrived at choosing the names on your list, the one thing they all have in common is how the development of their Life Palette became automatic. The fundamentals they put into place to create their Life Palette simply became a part of who they were. People like this would struggle to recall what they did or even how they learned to develop their palette. Sure, they had to work at it, just like I did when learning how to drive a stick shift. But ultimately they did it, and it forever defined who they were and the impact they had on others.

At the start, developing your Life Palette will be technical, frustrating, and even nerve racking. But as you practice the God-given principles set forth in this book, you'll live your life in such a way that the master artist can paint each day with the brush strokes of His creativity and destiny for you.

Living, like painting, is a process. Your Life Palette is a means to an end. Most people spend their life concentrating so much on earning a living and learning how to do their jobs or advance their careers, they miss out on living as the masterpiece they are created to be. It's in living as His masterpiece that you find joy, peace, purpose, and fulfillment. The process of developing the fundamentals and disciplines of your Life Palette will ultimately allow or limit you to live life fully and completely.

Proud of His masterpiece

Kevin McPherson is considered one of the top representational artists of our time. He is collected worldwide, exhibits in some of the best galleries in the United States, and is popular as a workshop teacher. I read that Kevin will sometimes keep one of his paintings because he feels he painted it just right. He knows that it is a masterpiece from his own hands, created from his palette. I imagine he frames it, hangs it on his wall, and celebrates its beauty with a sense of pride and joy. He knows it is an example of how his years and lifetime of work and discipline have paid off.

That's exactly how God feels about you. He is the artist. He has created you and declared that you are His masterpiece. Picture Him framing and displaying you in His heavenly gallery, proudly declaring you to be one of His best works of art.

Ready to start developing your Life Palette? Just like an artist preparing to paint, the process begins with a look at the values you're going to use—and how those values show up on the canvas of your life.

Palette Points

1. It's important to see yourself as God's masterpiece. Revisit Ephesians 2:10, apply it to memory, and make it personal: "For we are (I am) God's masterpiece. He has created us (me) anew in Christ Jesus, so we (I) can do the good things he planned for us (me) long ago."

2. Consider the three attitude checks to clean and begin preparing your Life Palette:

   - Are there areas of your life where you blame God? If so, take a moment, confess them to Him, and ask Him to help you change from this moment on.

   - Are you worried about what others think? How can you begin today to trust God as the only one qualified to decide what makes you a masterpiece?

   - Do you completely trust that God knows what He's doing as the artist of your life? If no, why not? If yes, describe why.

3. In this book, the formula for success is: Living *daily* as the masterpiece God created you to be. How does this formula work with your current definition of success?

4. Who would you list as someone who has lived, or is living, their life as the masterpiece God created them to be? Why?

5. Your Life Palette determines how your life is lived as His masterpiece. Ask God to show you the choices you need to make right now to move forward creating your Life Palette. What is one thing you will do to begin?

My One Priority to begin:

My Action Plan:

LIFE PALETTE

CHAPTER 1
Up To The Rivers Edge
24 x 18"

Location: Yellowstone National Park

From the artist: I painted this painting after a trip to Yellowstone National Park. While Yellowstone is an amazing place, the preservation of the landscape and wildlife offer a chance to step back in time and experience the west in the days of mountain men and trappers. Living in the desert makes the abundance of water in Yellowstone very appealing to experience and paint. *Up To The Rivers Edge* was selected for a show called Paint The Parks Top 100 in 2012 and toured the country for a year during that show in several different galleries.

To view or purchase Jeff's art, check out www.jeffloveart.com

Life Palette

Chapter 2

Glory And Grandeur
18 x 36"
Location: Grand Teton National Park

From the artist: Few places have captured my attention and kept it like Grand Teton National Park. There are thousands of perfect compositions waiting to be painted in the park and surrounding Jackson Hole area. The evening sunlight highlighting the Teton peaks were a perfect moment that I captured on film, have done several studio pieces from, and plan to do several more.

Chapter 3
Boundless
24 x 36"

Location: Grand Canyon National Park

From the artist: The Grand Canyon will not be outdone by any of the National Parks when it comes to amazing and endless compositions to paint. As an Arizona artist, I am privileged to have the Grand Canyon in my backyard, so to speak. I'm always amazed at how many people who live in our state have never traveled to see this amazing wonder of the world, and even more surprised when I hear those who have seen it describe it as just a big hole in the ground. I always ask if they have hiked down in it, because being in the canyon is a life-changing experience. I not only paint the Grand Canyon. I have hiked it rim to rim and look forward to many more trips down to the Colorado River.

Life Palette

Chapter 4
Glacier Bend
12 x 24"

Location: Glacier National Park

From the artist: We recently traveled to Glacier National Park as a family and as always the easel goes with us. Finding a perfect spot for me to stop and do an *en plein air* painting is normal on our family trips. I painted *Glacier Bend* in the studio from studies and photo references a few weeks after returning home from our family Glacier trip. This specific spot in the park was way off the beaten path. We had decided to take a trip to the Canadian border and walk across in the wilderness, just to say we did. Along the way we found some of the most stunning scenes of the park. A river and mountain scene always appeals to me, but this one in particular had to be painted, knowing that so few people will ever see it in real life.

Chapter Two

Values, Values, Values

When we first moved to Tucson, Arizona from Texas, our family went through the uncomfortable necessity of finding a family physician. Being totally new to the city, I asked some of our new friends for their recommendations. I set up an appointment with one of the doctors whose name I was given.

It was my first and last visit.

When I went into his office, everything was very professional and the atmosphere was fine. I was immediately disappointed, though, when the doctor walked in to see me—because he was obese. Now, before you think I am prejudiced against people who are overweight, understand that I've had my own struggles in that area (I'm not sure why, but ice cream always tastes better in the middle of the night when I can't sleep). So it's not that I'm against overweight people at all, but I am against my personal physician telling me to watch my health and well-being when it's abundantly clear he doesn't value his own health. I recognize there are many who have weight issues for reasons that are beyond their control, but in my brief conversation with this physician, I realized that was not the case for him. He was preaching to me about diet and exercise while giving it no place of value in his own life.

If you don't live it, you don't value it. It reminds me of what my dad often said to me when I was growing up. I'd see him doing something he'd told me not to do, and he'd say, "Do as I say, not as I do." Maybe you had parents who said the same thing, or have said it to your children. Problem is, it doesn't work. What's really being said is, "I want you to value this, even though I don't."

To say we value something isn't enough; lip service does not prove we value anything. If we don't live what we say, we may think we value something, even though we don't. When talking to others about their values, it's easy to discover what they truly value. When someone says they value living a healthy lifestyle, a few quick questions will reveal the truth. "Do you exercise?" "Do you eat right?" If the answer is "No," they don't really value their health. They like the idea of it, but it's not a value because what we truly value is not only displayed in how we think but also how we live.

Are your values "off?"

Your values are vitally important to developing your Life Palette. I did a painting workshop at the Tucson Art Academy with an artist named Gabor Svagrik. I went home each night hearing Gabor's voice echoing the same key phrase in my mind. He stated it incessantly, and it was profoundly simple: "Values, values, values."

In painting, value has to do with dark and light. For instance, mountains in the distance appear lighter and bluer than mountains that are closer to you. An example of this is the painting in this book, "Glory and Grandeur." The values cause the mountains to look as if they are at different distances, yet we all know that it is a one-dimensional painting.

If an artist reverses the values, they will appear to be reversed in the painting. In other words, the mountains that are supposed to appear far away and distant will look like they are very close to the viewer. When an artist sees that the value of the distant mountains is too dark, they'll say it needs to be "pushed back"—that is, the mountains need to be made to look like they're further away. Anytime that happens the values of the painting are said to be "off." If the color values are off, so is the entire painting. Everyone can see it. You may not be a trained artist or able to put it into words, but if the values are wrong in a painting, you'll know it and you won't like the painting because of it.

The same is true with your Life Palette. When your values don't line up with God's values as defined in Scripture, you end up working against Him as He paints on the canvas of your life. He's working on a masterpiece, but the values you're placing on your Life Palette may be limiting the look of your canvas to a cheap, drugstore painting, a "Velvet Elvis," when it should be not only better than a "Velvet Elvis," but a masterpiece.

In his book *Fill Your Oil Painting with Light & Color*, artist Kevin McPherson says, "Many students say they have trouble finishing a piece, but most often the problem lies at the start of their painting process. Most people can't finish because their foundation has not been properly laid." The foundation of your life is your values, and they must be established as a core of who you are and all you do. If you don't feel you've "properly laid" your values, the good news is God will give you the chance to start fresh and new.

> **Our Life Palette is a series of choices and decisions that ultimately determine if our lives reflect the masterpiece God designed us to be.**

Setting your values foundation

The Bible gives us direction on a variety of key values that should be forefront in our lives, and we'll review them shortly. But there is one value that we *must* get right. It's not one I've made up or discovered on my own; it comes from Jesus Christ Himself, and here it is:

> "Seek the Kingdom of God above all else, and live righteously, and he will give you everything you need."
> (Matthew 6:33)

Since God is the one who has created us as masterpieces, it's logical that we make Him and His kingdom our top priority and the foundational core value in our lives.

What is your primary concern in life? What is it you are pursuing above everything else? When you answer these questions, you will discover your core foundational value. The masterpiece of your life will never rise above your core foundational value, so it's imperative your top priority be something that will last and be something of worth. When you make the Kingdom of God your primary concern, all of your other values will align with it, and you can be assured that your life will be the masterpiece God intended it to be.

What is the "Kingdom of God?" Simply put, it's the "authority, will, or rule of God." To live righteously is to take on the righteousness or character of Jesus. It's the greatest purpose of any human; we were created for God's will. We were created as objects of His love, to love Him, serve Him, worship Him, and have a relationship with Him; in doing so, we reflect His will and character—His kingdom—in our lives. It's the place of greatest freedom and ultimate fulfillment.

Between the Palette Scrapings with Phil Starke

In painting, values are foundational. If the values are off in a painting, you scrape it and start over.

The story of two sisters, Mary and Martha, gives us a real life snapshot of what it means to make the Kingdom of God your primary concern. It's found in Luke 10:38-42, and the setting is a dinner party for a very important guest, Jesus. I can't even imagine what kind of preparations I'd be doing (okay, my wife would be doing) if the Lord were coming over to my house for dinner. To say I'd be distracted would be a bit of an understatement.

As any good hostess worth her salt, Martha went above and beyond what was needed for her guest of honor, and she was certainly distracted by it all. You can hardly blame her, yet I can't help but wonder, "What was Martha's primary concern?" Could it be her attention to the details of throwing a grand party and serving her guest an incredible dinner was more for *her* glory than for Jesus' benefit?

Mary, on the other hand, spent her time sitting at Jesus' feet listening to what He had to say. Her desire was to learn all she could from Christ while He was in her home. Her primary concern was the relationship she had with Jesus. Martha, frustrated that her sister wasn't doing anything to help her with dinner preparations, complained to Christ. Funny, isn't it? Here's Martha, whining to the guest of honor about how she wasn't getting help in preparing for whom? The guest of honor. It's downright convoluted.

Jesus' response was merciful yet direct. "My dear Martha, you are so upset over all these details! There is really only one thing worth being concerned about. Mary has discovered it—and I won't take it away from her." (Luke 10:41-42)

Jesus confirmed Mary's value was right and good—and properly prioritized. Seeking Him was her primary concern, and according to Jesus, it must be yours as well.

Primary concern, primary changes

When Jesus said to Martha, "There is really only one thing worth being concerned about," He gave us a secret that's simple, powerful, and profound: to have "one thing," or one primary concern. This is the core value for every other value on your Life Palette. Get this one right and your chances of success in everything you do is multiplied beyond your wildest dreams. Paul said, "Now all glory to God, who is able, through his mighty power at work within us, to accomplish infinitely more than we might ask or think." (Ephesians 4:20) I love it! More than you think or imagine? Yes, more! Paul gives us a verbal picture of what our lives look like when we live as the masterpiece we're created to be.

When we hear Jesus' words to Martha and read Paul's words in Ephesians, the question we often ask is how? How do I make the

Kingdom of God my primary concern, the foundational core value on my Life Palette? As is often true in many areas of our lives, the problem is that we're asking the wrong question. The question is not "how," but "who." Don't miss the power of Jesus' response to Martha as her sister Mary sits at His feet: "There is really only one thing worth being concerned about. Mary has discovered it."

God's design for your life as a masterpiece begins with Jesus as the foundational core value on your Life Palette. Paul tells us, "Since you have been raised to new life with Christ, set your sights on the realities of heaven, where Christ sits in the place of honor at God's right hand." (Colossians 3:1) When we make the choice of receiving "new life in Christ," He will lead us to all of the other core values necessary on our Life Palette, helping us to get them right for our lives now—and ultimately for our future that's "more than we might ask or think." There are several primary changes that will take place on your Life Palette when you do this.

First, you will begin to **exchange your priorities for Jesus' priorities**. Paul tells you to "think about the things of heaven, not the things of earth." (Colossians 3:2) In another scripture, Paul says to "fix your thoughts on what is true, and honorable, and right, and pure, and lovely, and admirable. Think about things that are excellent and worthy of praise." (Philippians 4:8) He is clarifying what life in Jesus looks like. Each of you will have different priorities in your life according to your personality, gifts, family, and daily responsibilities; yet there are several priorities of Christ that should be guarded and cultivated to allow God to continue to create your life as a masterpiece. We will discuss these more in the next chapter as we look at Jesus' values, and in chapter five as we talk about your priorities on your Life Palette.

The second change to occur when you make the Kingdom of God your primary concern is that **you get His perspective**. "For you died to this life, and your real life is hidden with Christ in God." (Colossians 3:3) When you die to self, you get a new perspective about all of life. Maybe you've heard stories of someone who had a near-death experience and they talk about how they see life differently now. When you choose to follow Mary's example and get your core value of your Life Palette to line up with what Jesus said, you will die to this life.

I can't imagine anyone who understood this concept better than Lazarus, Christ's dear friend and brother of Mary and Martha. His story is found in John 11. According to the witnesses in the New Testament, Lazarus died—and by the time Jesus arrived on the scene, the sisters had given him a funeral and he'd been in his grave for four days. Enough time has passed that when Jesus told them to remove the stone sealing the entrance to Lazarus' grave, Martha protested, "Lord the smell will be terrible." Then Jesus brought him back to life! Apparently, God was not done with His masterpiece named Lazarus.

Imagine how differently Lazarus looked at his life after being dead for four days. He surely understood what it was like to have died to this life and be hidden in Christ. Everything in his world would've been different. He was seeing things through a perspective that only a dead man could see. That's the place of true masterpiece living potential!

The third change of making the Kingdom of God your primary concern is having a **change in your attitude**. We'll look at some attitudes to work on for your Life Palette a little later. Here, I'm talking about how your overall attitude of life becomes like Jesus' attitude. Paul said at the beginning of Colossians 3:4: "And when Christ, who is your life…" Notice he didn't say when Christ gets a special compartment of your life. This line screams the primary core value of your Life Palette; "And when Christ, who *is* your life…" The primary attitude of your life changes as dramatically as a man who was dead for four days and was suddenly brought back to life! He was as you should be—a dead man walking; "for you died to this life, and your real life is hidden with Christ in God."

Values God wants on every Life Palette

Throughout the Bible there are several values God tells us are His will for all of us. We don't need to pray about whether or not we want them on our Life Palette; He tells us He wants us to make sure they *are* on our Life Palette. We simply need to develop our understanding and cultivate our use of them.

1. The Holy Spirit. Paul tells us in Ephesians 5:18 that we are to "be filled with the Holy Spirit." In Galatians, he encourages us to "follow the Spirit's leading in every part of our lives." (Galatians 5:25)

2. Pray consistently. Ephesians 6:18 says, "Pray in the Spirit at all times and on every occasion. Stay alert and be persistent in your prayers for all believers everywhere." In other words, prayer should be a lifestyle.

3. Thankfulness. I once looked up every verse in the Bible on giving thanks. A stack of pages emerged from the printer, back when all we had were those noisy dot matrix printers. Don't take my word for it. Do a word study and you will come to the same conclusion: giving thanks is to be a value on every person's Life Palette. "And whatever you do or say, do it as a representative of the Lord Jesus, giving thanks through him to God the Father." (Colossians 3:17)

4. Rejoice always. "Always be full of joy in the Lord. I say it again—rejoice!" (Philippians 4:4) This is not an option. We are to proclaim His glory and His praise. We will all go about it differently and express it in our own way according to our God-given personalities and gifts, but rejoicing is to be on every Life Palette.

5. Submit to authorities. Really? I grew up in a time when you often saw the bumper sticker that said "Question Authority." I was only a kid in the 1960s, but the teenagers I admired and wanted to be like were all about making sure you didn't submit to anyone! Yet God, the artist of our lives, says this is an essential part of living as a masterpiece. Jesus gave us an example when asked about paying taxes: "'Now tell us what you think about this: Is it right to pay taxes to Caesar or not?' But Jesus knew their evil motives. 'You hypocrites!' he said. 'Why are you trying to trap me? Here, show me the coin used for the tax.' When they handed him a Roman coin, he asked, 'Whose picture and title are stamped on it?' 'Caesar's,' they replied. 'Well, then,' he said, 'give to Caesar what belongs to Caesar, and give to God what belongs to God.'" (Matthew 22:17-21)

I love how Jesus began His answer, "Well, then…" It's as though He was giving an answer that we often find in our modern culture:

"Duh!" You may question at this point, "What if an authority says to do something against God's Word?" Look to the life of Peter and John when they were told to quit talking about Jesus. "But Peter and John replied, 'Do you think God wants us to obey you rather than him? We cannot stop telling about everything we have seen and heard.'" (Acts 4:19-20) And who did they obey? "They called in the apostles (Peter and John) and had them flogged. Then they ordered them never again to speak in the name of Jesus, and they let them go. The apostles left the high council rejoicing that God had counted them worthy to suffer disgrace for the name of Jesus. And every day, in the Temple and from house to house, they continued to teach and preach this message: 'Jesus is the Messiah.'" (Acts 5:40-42)

6. Purity. God's will is for us to be pure, and this includes staying away from sexual sin. Why would God make this a value for each of us as a masterpiece? Simple. He created sex and knows completely the incredible intimacy, joy, and pleasure that by design it brings to a marriage. He also understands that when we do not live in the value of sexual purity, it will destroy intimacy, steal our joy, and cause us to pursue worldly pleasure—all of which are things the enemy wants to use to destroy God's masterpiece. While all sin is sin and will take away the worth of our lives, Paul tells us this one has a different impact on us than others: "Run from sexual sin! No other sin so clearly affects the body as this one does. For sexual immorality is a sin against your own body." (1 Corinthians 6:18-19)

I need to pray for God to help me to avoid sexual immorality and be pure, but do I need to pray about whether or not I should consider making sexual sin a part of my life? No. He's made it clear He wants purity to be a value on everyone's Life Palette. "Food was made for the stomach, and the stomach for food. (This is true, though someday God will do away with both of them.) But you can't say that our bodies were made for sexual immorality. They were made for the Lord, and the Lord cares about our bodies." (1 Corinthians 6:13-14)

As a pastor, I've never had someone come into my office and tell me that one of the greatest things they've done in their lives is give in to sexual immorality. No one has ever told me it has added value to their lives, or that it has allowed them to shine as God's masterpiece. However, I could share with you hundreds of stories of brokenness, hurt, shame, and regret because of it.

My list is not intended to be all-inclusive from the Bible, but rather a statement of the obvious as you read the Scriptures and look at the life of Jesus and the disciples. When you choose to make the Kingdom of God your primary concern, you take the first step to living as the masterpiece God created you to be. Perhaps some of the values I've listed are not currently on your Life Palette. Perhaps you sense God speaking to you. Don't hesitate. Act now. Ask God to give you wisdom in these areas and commit to Him that, as His masterpiece, you are willing to choose to make His values your values. Ask Him for His help, courage, and power to begin to live them out. Then begin to grow in your understanding of each of them through the Bible and begin to cultivate each of them onto your Life Palette.

> **If you don't live it, you don't value it.**

What we really want to know

When I was a kid, the questions of life were easy. "Why is the sky blue?" "Do all dogs go to heaven?" "Why can't I have more ice cream?" But as I got older the questions changed. They got harder. "Where should I go to college? "Is she 'the one?'" "God, what do you want me to do with my life?" In other words, "Lord, what's your will?"

Our Life Palette is a series of choices and decisions that ultimately determine if our lives reflect the masterpiece God designed us to be. We've all made some really good decisions, some really bad ones, and some really dumb ones. The more we come to know and understand God's will for our lives, the more we can live in the really good ones. "Be very careful, then, how you live—not as unwise but as wise, making the most of every opportunity, because the days are evil. Therefore do not be foolish, but understand what the Lord's will is." (Ephesians 5:15-17 NIV)

God's will is not a mystery that He's hiding from you. He wants you to know and understand His will. He's not sitting in heaven playing some cruel game just to keep you guessing. Quite the contrary—He is doing everything in His power to communicate His will for you to live as His masterpiece. Often the problem is you're simply looking for the wrong thing. To make the Kingdom of God your primary concern, you need to be able to understand the will of the King so you can discern and discover His will for you.

First, **God's will is not an emotion**. So often we're simply looking for a feeling, a wave of emotions to come over us, especially if we're right-brained creative types. (I'm speaking to myself right now!) The problem is emotions can take us in the opposite direction of His will. We'd all like to have the emotional response that comes with a supernatural sign for every decision. If the Lord would only give us a burning bush like He gave Moses, surely none of us would ever get off track.

I live in the desert southwest where we have some of the greatest Mexican food in the world. Sometimes my emotions get dictated by the burrito I had the night before, not by God. It may not be the burrito for you—but it could be fatigue, hormones, an event you just experienced, or a movie you recently saw that particularly moved you. Our emotions are very unreliable and not trustworthy when it comes to answering the big question of God's will. It's too important for masterpiece living to be left up to the burrito from last night's supper.

Second, **God's will is not a recipe**. Living as God's masterpiece is not simply a logical, rational thing. Perhaps you're more of a left-brained person and you're looking for the step-by-step formula that always works to know and live by God's will. What you really want are all the procedures and systems that lead you to it. Yet a formula or recipe has to be perfect each and every time; there is no room for failure. God has allowed us, in all of our humanity and with all of our fumbles and failures, to be His masterpiece.

When I was a kid I loved applesauce cake. I'm not sure why. Perhaps it was because we had plenty of fresh apples growing on my grandparents' farm. I loved it so much that my mother taught me to make it for myself and I did quite often. (Mom may have thought this would make me want to bake or cook, but that didn't take!) Once I was at my grandparents' home for supper and I wanted applesauce cake for dessert, so grandma told me to make one, and I did. But I forgot one ingredient: sugar. It was horrible. No one would eat it. My grandparents' faithful farm dog, the one who devoured all the leftovers, wouldn't even eat it.

If God's will were a formula, your life as a masterpiece would be worthless if you left out even one simple ingredient. There would be no room for failure or errors. God's will is a part of the relationship He wants to have with us as His sons and daughters. Like any relationship, it is dynamic. The problem for us is that the freedom found in this dynamic will of God can often be the very thing that gives us consternation. The better we get to know Him and the more we develop our relationship with Him, the more we will know His will in the daily decisions of our lives. My wife and I have been married for nearly 30 years now, and every once in a while we will tell a story from our childhood that the other has never heard before. We're still getting to know one another. It's part of the joy and wonder of a relationship. Plus, the more we grow in our relationship and the more we know about one another, the more we are able to love each other and meet each other's needs. The same is true in our relationship with God.

Don't be afraid to ask God to guide you in His will. Arrogance will keep you from living life as His masterpiece. God wants to give you direction for this journey. Jesus' brother James wrote this: "If you need wisdom, ask our generous God, and he will give it to you. He will not rebuke you for asking. But when you ask him, be sure that your faith is in God alone. Do not waver, for a person with divided loyalty is as unsettled as a wave of the sea that is blown and tossed by the wind." (James 1:5-6)

God desires to communicate His will. That's all a part of why He sent Jesus to the earth, to get up close and personal with us as human beings. That's why He gave us the Bible, His Word. Some things are very clear, like the values we listed earlier; others are principles that He wants us to live by.

What is it that you already know you are supposed to do, but haven't done yet? You may just be waiting, but delayed obedience is disobedience. If there is even one thing you know you should do, or that

He is leading you to do that you're putting it off, do it now. Don't let it be something that keeps you from living as His masterpiece. Obedience is another one of those values He wants on your Life Palette. "If you love me," Jesus said. "obey my commandments." (John 14:15)

Not all value expressions are the same

I love to join other artists and paint *en plein air*, a simple term taken from the French meaning "to paint outside." What's interesting is how several artists can paint the same landscape and still create such different pictures. One of the key things that make each painting unique is how each artist paints the values of the landscape; that is, the darks and lights used as the painting's foundation.

Between the Palette Scrapings with Phil Starke

Artists fall in love with colors. That's what we love. But values are what is important. Values make colors work. Values set up a painting for success; without the right values, there is no hope of creating a masterpiece.

The master artist, God, does the same thing with our Life Palette. We're each uniquely created with a variety of God-given desires for pursuing and accomplishing our destinies, so while the source of our values is the same (the Bible), the way those values are specifically played out in our lives will often be different.

Take priorities for example. Before my wife Kathy and I got married, we decided that we'd make choices in our lifestyle to allow us to live on my income only. It wasn't that she couldn't work, but we wanted to be in a financial position where, when we had children, she'd have the option of being a stay-at-home mom. This was an extension of a "family before career" core value we felt was important for us and remains that way to this day. As a pastor, I have guarded this very carefully over the years, making sure our kids do not feel that church would ever come before them. After all, we feel the people we are given the greatest responsibility to disciple are our children.

Over the years we have enjoyed the benefits of our decision. Kathy did earn a teaching degree and has taught in a few different schools for short periods of time. But for most of our married life, she has felt compelled to use her teaching degree to home school our children. This was something she could never have done, regardless of how strongly she felt about it, had we not based our lifestyle on our values.

> *God's design for your life as a masterpiece begins with Jesus as the foundational core value on your Life Palette.*

With each value we choose, there are pros and cons. Our decision to live on one income meant we chose to live in a smaller, older home. It meant that while most of our friends had two cars, we shuffled our lives and schedules around one. Yet we've never regretted the decision because it allowed us to live our family values as a couple. Remember, though, that the specific way I live out my values can't be yours and yours can't be mine. To do that would make you nothing more than a forgery, a cheap imitation. That's not God's plan. You are an original one-of-a-kind masterpiece. Therefore, the expression of many of your values will be unique to you and your situation.

Take a Closer Look

Establishing your core values for your Life Palette is absolutely essential. Take the biblical guidelines you've been given in this chapter and prayerfully consider them. If you don't go through the spiritual struggle of spelling out your values and how you'll live them out, you will find yourself unconsciously living the world's values, be it from the latest Hollywood movie to keeping up with the Joneses. You'll find yourself blown and tossed about like a boat at sea without a rudder. Scripture warns "people like that should not expect to receive anything from the Lord. They can't make up their minds. They waver back and forth in everything they do." (James 1:7-8)

You face value choices every day in your life. Much like in painting, if something is not quite right, the artist reassesses the core values of the picture. If your life is out of balance or even out of control, and you know it's not looking like the masterpiece God created you to be, take a look at your values and how you are living them out. What choices are you making daily that are not in line with your core values?

Next, we'll look at how Jesus lived with the Kingdom of God as His primary concern, and how we can follow His example as we develop our Life Palette.

Palette Points

1. List at least three values you have in your life (true values you live):

2. Are there things you say you value, but after reading this chapter you've discovered you *like* the idea of them, but have not truly made them values? What are they and why?

3. Are there values on your Life Palette you believe could prove harmful if you continue to value them? What are they and what do you need to do about them right now?

4. Consider the values listed that God desires on every Life Palette—the Holy Spirit, praying consistently, being thankful, rejoicing always, submitting to authorities, and purity. Which of these do you need to make a value on your Life Palette? How?

5. Take a few moments and look at Matthew 6:33. What do you need to do to make the Kingdom of God your primary concern?

My One Priority regarding my values:

My Action Plan:

Chapter Three

A Valuable Example

If you want to be kept honest about your values, look no further than the minds of children. There's no fooling them. You can't get away with telling them one thing and then living it out differently without being called to the carpet on it and held accountable.

When my son Joel was young, my office was in our home (it was actually just a desk in the garage, but "office" sure sounded better). There are few things I miss about those days in my garage, not the least of which were the hot desert summers without air conditioning and 100 degree temperatures, or the occasional cold winter day without a heater. But one thing I do miss about my home office was being around my family all the time, even if I was easily distracted by their presence. I couldn't resist those times when Joel interrupted my preparation for the weekend talk with, "Daddy, would you please play with me?"

Joel often wandered into the garage to get my attention. As he talked, I'd murmur an occasional "Uh-huh" while never looking away from the computer screen. I was trying to stay focused on what I was working on, but I didn't want to ignore my son, either—a value conflict for sure. Joel wouldn't have it. He kept me honest. The moment he felt I was only appeasing him, Joel grabbed my face with both of his hands. He then turned my head and forced me to look him right in the eyes. "Dad!" he said. "You're not listening to me." That always got my attention. Why? I value being a great father to my children. I value their lives and want to give them my best. Joel kept me honest. I couldn't casually "Uh-huh" my way around being an attentive dad.

As Joel grew older, he knew he was a priority in my life. I've learned to look him straight in the eye when we talk. He's also learned that part of my being a great father to him is living out my God-given destiny by doing my work with excellence. That means there are times that Joel needs to wait. He understands that I'm not doing this because I'm ignoring him, but that I simply have to finish what I'm focused on first.

I can only have this perspective when my core value of making the Kingdom of God my primary concern is on my Life Palette. The balance of work, family life, and daily demands is made clearer because of it. With the Kingdom of God as my top priority, I can be the dad my kids need me to be and love them the way I desire. I can love my wife the way I should and be the husband I desire to be. I can live out my God-given purpose through my work.

Being honest with yourself and God

Just as Joel has kept me honest, we all need to be honest with ourselves about what we're making our primary pursuit in life. For some it may be approval, money, progress, order, organization, or any array of things. They may all be good, healthy things; but if any of these take first priority or are in conflict with the Kingdom of God, they will ultimately stand in the way of God painting our lives into a masterpiece.

Another problem with making anything besides the Kingdom of God primary in your life is that there's never a finish line to any earthly thing. Have you noticed this, too? If you're living for approval, you will never get to the place where you feel you have acceptance. If its money, how much do you need before you can say you have enough and will no longer seek more? Ecclesiastes 5:10 affirms, "Those who love money will never have enough. How absurd to think that wealth brings true happiness!" It's not that these things are necessarily bad. God celebrates these gifts in your life. He intended them for your good, but they can't be first ahead of Him. When you discover that you have allowed something to trump first place in your life, you'll also soon discover that your life, designed to be a masterpiece, is instead looking oddly like a forgery.

Type A personalities, the go-getters of life, may think prioritizing God's Kingdom above more "practical" demands of life sounds complacent, even non-productive. Nothing could be further from the truth. Getting this core foundational value right is not about sitting around on your hands and never getting anything done. God created you with drive, dreams, and destiny. Yet if they become your primary pursuit, you'll soon find that they drive you instead of you driving them. The very things the Lord gave you as good gifts will ultimately become distractions from being the masterpiece God desires.

Once you're honest with yourself and with God about your life's core value, you'll discover a lie lurks behind any value or belief that does not line up with God's Word. Perhaps you don't believe you can trust God with your finances because you believe His ways of handling money and possessions are antiquated, not current with culture. Yet Paul tells you the truth in Philippians 4:19: "And this same God who takes care of me will supply all your needs from his glorious riches, which have been given to us in Christ Jesus." Why wouldn't you trust Him completely and obey Him in this area? The lurking lie is that He won't *really* supply all your needs, and you're on your own. Or maybe you feel God could never be pleased with you as His child because you never pleased your parents while growing up. You raised your grade in math from a C to a B and their response was, "If you really applied yourself, you could get an A."

Whatever it is, the lurking lie often leads us to sin. We believe the sin tempting us will give us an outcome different than what God's Word says it will bring. Our value is all wrong. Much like an artist who begins a painting with the wrong values, all the color in the world will not fix it. The artist may try fancy brush strokes and applying advanced techniques, but without correcting the core value the painting will never be quite right.

Look to Jesus as the example

We can certainly look to the example of other godly men and women from our past or in our lives today to show us how to make God's Kingdom our primary concern. But I suggest looking to a standard both human and divine, the one who fully lived His life on earth according to the values of heaven—Jesus Christ. His life and words give you perfect insight on how to make the Kingdom of God your primary concern.

Jesus expressed His core foundational value in three particular ways. This is not intended to be an all-inclusive list from Christ's life, but as you model your life after this trio, you'll create a Life Palette with which God can paint the canvas of your life as the masterpiece He created you to be.

1. Relationships

Jesus valued relationships. In Mark 12, Jesus and His disciples were in the temple courts surrounded by a crowd. The religious leaders of His day were asking questions and discussing Jesus' answers. They were literally debating. One of the religious leaders thought Christ's answers were profound, so he pressed in and asked Jesus which commandment was the most important. Jesus' response was all about relationships, first with God and then with others. "The most important commandment is this: 'Listen, O Israel! The LORD our God is the one and only LORD. And you must love the LORD your God with all your heart, all your soul, all your mind, and all your strength.' The second is equally important: 'Love your neighbor as yourself.' No other commandment is greater than these." (Mark 12:29-31)

As you choose to make relationship with God and others a key expression of your core foundational value, you will have favor with God and will see amazing changes in those relationships, including your relationship with God. In Luke 2, we see the relational interaction Jesus had with His parents when He was 12 years old. His family had traveled to Jerusalem for the Passover festival. Afterward Mary and Joseph headed home, believing their son was traveling among those making the journey with them. When Jesus didn't show up at camp that evening, they headed back to Jerusalem to look for Him. They searched three days before finding Him in the temple among the religious leaders, listening to their teachings and asking questions. Mary knew the true identity of her son, yet her reaction was typical of any parent who has spent three days looking for a lost child. "'Son!' his mother said to him. 'Why have you done this to us? Your father and I have been frantic, searching for you everywhere.'" (Luke 2:48) And it's clear Jesus knew His true identity by His response: "'But why did you need to search?' he asked. 'Didn't you know that I must be in my Father's house?'" (Luke 2:49)

I was 12 years old a long time ago. As a parent I've had four 12 year olds, so I understand that when you're that age, one of the hardest tasks is obeying your parents. No one then believes "father knows best." You feel like *you* know what is best and therefore should be running your world as you see fit. And yet when Jesus is tempted to be a typical 12 year old, we see Him putting into practice the biblical principle of loving God and loving others—that is, making relationships with God and others part of His core values. How do we know that? We see the end of the story: "Then he returned to Nazareth with them and was obedient to them. And his mother stored all these things in her heart. Jesus grew in wisdom and in stature and in favor with God and all the people." (Luke 2:51-52)

Don't miss the last few words. They give us insight into Jesus modeling relationships as a value for making the Kingdom of God His primary concern. As a result, He grew mentally, spiritually, and physically, in favor with God the Father and with other people. He began modeling for us the importance of relationships on our Life Palette many years before He even began His earthly ministry.

The Investment

What is the cost of valuing relationships? It's the investment of time—by far the most priceless gift we have to give. Relationships take time, yet our culture and fast pace of living can quickly push our schedules to the limit and cause us to diminish or even put off relationships. Healthy, productive relationships with God and others are dependent on the *margin* of time we have to invest in them.

During one of our Durango, Colorado vacations our family decided that we would drive across the famed "Million Dollar Highway" to visit some friends who live in that area. The road earned its name because many people will tell you that you could not pay them a million dollars to drive it again because of its mountainous path and curious lack of guard rails.

During this trip on the highway we ran into a torrential rain storm. As we neared the summit of the pass the rain turned to sleet. The road was slick and it was hard to see. There are several spots on that drive where there is no margin for error; cross the white line and you will plummet down the side of the mountain. Driving there in normal conditions is stressful enough; during a storm, it's downright miserable. After crowning the pass and heading down the northern slopes, we were met with a couple of mudslides that left us stranded on the highway for several hours. Still, I love the area and will definitely make the drive again, but preferably in better weather.

Relationships without a margin of time investment is a lot like driving the "Million Dollar Highway" during an unexpected mountain storm. You may make it to the other side, but the journey can be miserable. That is not God's intent for your relationship with Him or with others.

Between the Palette Scrapings with Phil Starke

Rembrandt is a good example of painting values. He used a very limited palette of black, red, and yellow, and then added a little color. Values were his foundation. Many modern artists make colors or a political statement more important than their values, and the results are often a garish painting.

Over the years of serving in ministry I have stood beside many beds as people prepared to take their final breath. I have never heard one person say that they wish they had spent more time at the office or invested more time making money. I have, however, heard many speak words of regret about spending so little time with their families, their children, and their friends. That sorrow is only worsened by the desire to have had a deeper relationship with God.

One of the things Jesus valued is He chose relationship over reputation. In Matthew 11, Christ was willing to allow His reputation to be soiled by the religious leaders when He chose to have relationships with sinners. "The Son of Man, on the other hand, feasts and drinks, and you say, 'He's a glutton and a drunkard, and a friend of tax collectors and other sinners!'" (Matthew 11:19) I'm glad Jesus wore this as a badge of honor. Part of building the value of the Kingdom of God as our primary concern on our Life Palette is being willing to risk reputation for relationship. When we do, there will be times when we will be slandered, but we will also gain favor with God and others—and we'll see amazing changes happen in our relationships, and perhaps even see people come to know Jesus as Lord.

God created you with drive, dreams, and destiny.

2. Service

Jesus valued serving. We see throughout the Bible that being a servant was important to Christ. In living out service as a value on our Life Palette, we will discover freedom and live in it. At first glance it seems counterintuitive; we think of service as not living in freedom, but in bondage. Yet the most freeing thing we can do is live in submission to God.

One of the hardest things for a novice artist to learn is to paint with freedom. In the art world it's talked about as being "tight." As an artist, we need to learn to loosen up. One way I've tried to teach other artists to do this is by telling them the painting they're about to start will be thrown away. It's just practice; you can't keep it at the end. It's amazing how much freedom an artist has when they realize the painting is not going up on their mantle over the fireplace displayed for all to see. Personally, painting sunsets loosens me up. "Boundless" (see first color page section) is one of my favorites of the Grand Canyon sunset. The colors and sky change so quickly that I'm forced to paint fast and loose.

When service becomes a value on our Life Palette, our lives become "a living and holy sacrifice—the kind he (God) will find acceptable. This is truly the way to worship him." (Romans 12:1) It's a place of absolute freedom and the making of a masterpiece. It's releasing God as the artist to paint with freedom and create whatever He desires. It is in serving that we truly realize our lives are a canvas and God is the artist.

Absolute freedom

A servant understands five things about freedom and service.

First, **his time is not his own.** Imagine for a moment that a canvas could come to life and argue about the amount of time the artist wishes to spend to create his masterpiece. It's absurd, yet how many times have we done that with God as the artist of our lives? There is so much freedom in knowing the timetable is in His hands, and that as I stay within the rhythm of His grace for my life He will complete the masterpiece right on time. Jesus showed this in John 2. It's His first recorded miracle. Jesus and His mother Mary were guests at a wedding. They ran out of wine and Mary let Jesus know what had happened. His response gives us a picture of how He understood that He, too, was here to serve the Father—and how a servant's time was not His own. "'Dear woman, that's not our problem,' Jesus replied. 'My time has not yet come.'" (John 2:4) It was a phrase Jesus repeated several times throughout the New Testament.

Second, a servant understands **he has no choice but obedience.** We would again find it absurd to think a canvas would argue with the color placement or the brush stroke of the artist. Yet how often have we argued with God as the master artist because we didn't want to obey His will? In Mark 14:36, Jesus prayed "Abba, Father...everything is possible for you. Please take this cup of suffering away from me. Yet I want your will to be done, not mine." Christ modeled that, as a servant, there is no choice but obedience. It is the place of unbelievable freedom—to be able to put aside the end we think may happen, and know He is the artist and is in control of the end result.

Third, a servant **owns nothing.** At first, this may seem like a bad thing, but in reality it's quite the opposite; again, it is a place of incredible freedom. The owner is responsible for the upkeep and provision. God the Father takes full responsibility for our lives as His masterpiece, so much so that He was willing to send His Son to the cross to die for our sins.

I once traveled with several men from our church to a conference in Portland, Oregon. Most of them had never been in the Pacific Northwest, so I was excited to show them around during our off time. Knowing we would only be about an hour and a half from the coast, we rented a van to drive to the ocean. If you've ever rented a vehicle, you know they always ask if you want insurance on the rental. My response this time was, "I want enough insurance that if this van catches on fire, we can pull over beside the road, let it burn, and you'll bring us another van." I was half joking—but made it very clear we were planning on doing as much driving as we could. On our first free day, we took off to see the sights. As we were driving, everyone in the van kept saying they smelled something burning, playing off my comments at the rental counter. Yet there was an actual smell, and it was so strong we eventually stopped along the highway and walked around the van in search of its source. As far as we could tell, everything was normal. When we arrived at our first stop, the smell had increased so much we were sure

Between the Palette Scrapings with Phil Starke

Think value first and the right color will follow.

something was really burning. Then, as I went to set the emergency brake, I realized I had never released it when we left our hotel. We had a great laugh and, of course, I may never live down that mistake.

But here's the thing. I wasn't too bothered by the fact I was burning up the brakes on that van because I wasn't the owner and I had paid for insurance to make sure I would never be responsible for any damage or maintenance. That's the beauty of being a servant. The servant is never the owner. I'm not saying as a servant we should abuse the things of our master; on the contrary, good stewardship is vital. But for our Life Palette, we don't get to stand at the counter with God and tell Him we want insurance just in case we get a little careless.

Fourth, a servant **cannot compare his work with others.** Can you picture walking through an art museum full of masterpieces painted by different artists and one canvas speaks to the other, "Your colors are not as brilliant as my colors. Your composition is not as good as my composition. You're not the masterpiece I am." Again, it's absurd. Yet we often compare ourselves to others, forgetting God has created each of us as His individual masterpiece to uniquely reflect His glory and give Him honor. It's not our place to compare ourselves to others. Paul said, "Pay careful attention to your own work, for then you will get the satisfaction of a job well done, and you won't need to compare yourself to anyone else. For we are each responsible for our own conduct." (Galatians 6:4-5)

As you choose to make relationship with God and others a key expression of your core foundational value, you will have favor with God.

As an artist I understand this all too well. Every time I've been to a workshop, the first day everyone is concerned about how they compare to the other artists. There's always a sense of uneasiness, and you hope someone else in the room paints as badly as you think you paint. Usually everyone relaxes after they realize we're all there to learn, and that the only master artist among us is the one leading the workshop. When we compare ourselves with others, we also try to imitate them and quickly lose the unique touch God has given us. That's the freedom of being a servant. We're not the artist, and it's not about comparing the canvas of our lives with anyone else's. God's painting His one-of-a-kind masterpiece.

Fifth, a servant **has no worries**. It's an amazing place of freedom because the master takes care of everything. We often think being a servant is a negative thing, but its only negative if the servant's master is evil. When the master is good—or, more precise, when the master is God and perfect in every way—we can trust Him to meet all of our needs with no need for anxiety or concern. When I'm about to begin a painting, I carefully choose the canvas to place on my easel. It's important to me what kind of canvas it is: cotton, linen, or board. You may think it makes no difference. But an artist considers the masterpiece he has in mind and makes a careful choice of each canvas for the end result he desires. The painting is not worried about whether or not the artist is making the right choice. The artist is fully and completely responsible for choosing the type of canvas and for every brush stroke and every color on the canvas. No worries.

The Bible tells us, "Don't worry about anything; instead, pray about everything. Tell God what you need, and thank him for all he has done. Then you will experience God's peace, which exceeds anything we can understand. His peace will guard your hearts and minds as you live in Christ Jesus." (Philippians 4:6-7)

Don't worry about anything? That's right, because the master is the one responsible. That's why Paul tells us to replace worry with prayer and experience God's peace.

Leading the way

Jesus led the way in service. In John 13 we see an incredible scene as Christ gathers with His disciples for what we know as The Last Supper, the final meal before He was crucified. In the time of Christ, the servant of the household would always wash the guest's feet because they were dirty from walking on the dirt paths in sandals. Jesus clearly takes on the role of servant. "So he got up from the table, took off his robe, wrapped a towel around his waist, and poured water into a basin. Then he began to wash the disciples' feet, drying them with the towel he had around him." (John 13:4-5) After He was finished there's no misunderstanding of His desire for us to have servanthood as a value on our Life Palette. "After washing their feet, he put on his robe again and sat down and asked, 'Do you understand what I was doing? You call me 'Teacher' and 'Lord,' and you are right, because that's what I am. And since I, your Lord and Teacher, have washed your feet, you ought to wash each other's feet. I have given you an example to follow. Do as I have done to you. I tell you the truth, slaves are not greater than their master. Nor is the messenger more important than the one who sends the message. Now that you know these things, God will bless you for doing them.'" (John 13:12-17)

3. Sacrifice

The third value clearly seen in Jesus' life is sacrifice. It's a word none of us get excited about. I confess "sacrifice" is not a word I really like. It goes against my human nature. But to be the masterpiece God created me to be, the values on my Life Palette must line up with His values—even the ones I don't especially like.

No masterpiece has ever been painted without sacrifice. An artist does not wake up one day and simply paint. They began with a passion to create and invest time, resources, energy, and great effort to learn to paint. To the casual observer who watches an artist paint, they may say the artist makes it look so easy. But it only looks easy because they have sacrificed with years of practice. Thankfully, God as the artist of our life does not need to practice. He's perfect.

Still, Jesus led the way in sacrifice, too. In Mark 10 a wealthy man asked Jesus what he must do to inherit eternal life. As the dialogue unfolds, Jesus points toward the Ten Commandments. The rich man's response was that he'd kept all those commands, so Jesus said, "There is still one thing you haven't done…Go and sell all your possessions and give the money to the poor, and you will have treasure in heaven. Then come, follow me." (Mark 10:21) Sacrifice over wealth. It's not that Jesus is telling us we can't have money or things; He's saying money and things shouldn't have us. More than valuing the things of this world, we should value sacrifice. It's a part of every masterpiece.

In Matthew 5, Jesus also teaches us to value sacrifice by going beyond what's expected of us: "If someone wants to sue you and take your tunic, let him have your cloak as well. If someone forces you to go one mile, go with him two miles. Give to the one who asks you, and do not turn away from the one who wants to borrow from you." (Matthew 5:40-42 NIV) Jesus also challenges us to sacrifice and make a deposit into eternity. "Store your treasures in heaven, where moths and rust cannot destroy, and thieves do not break in and steal." (Matthew 6:20) And in the ultimate picture of how we are not the artist creating the masterpiece, Jesus says, "If you cling to your life, you will lose it; but if you give up your life for me, you will find it." (Matthew 10:39) Why would I value sacrifice like Jesus did? Why should it become a part of my Life Palette? Because in this value I find life; that is, I discover the rich, satisfying, fulfilling life as the masterpiece He created me to be.

> **No masterpiece has ever been painted without sacrifice.**

Remember, this is not an all-inclusive list of what Jesus values, but they are certainly three distinct values He lived out in His life and made clear we are to live out in ours. This is a good starting place for getting the right values on our Life Palette. However, God has created us as His unique masterpiece; therefore, we also have unique values He wants us to discover. It all starts in how we view them.

Palette Points

1. Looking to Jesus as your example, consider how you value these three key areas. Rate yourself on a scale of 1 to 10 (10 being Jesus).

   - Relationships
   - Service
   - Sacrifice

2. Why did you give yourself the rating you did with each value? What choices do you need to make right now to move yourself closer to Jesus on the scale?

3. Of the five things a servant understands about freedom, which one appeals to you most and why?

   - Time is not his own
   - No choice but obedience
   - Owns nothing
   - Cannot compare his work with others
   - Has no worries

4. Are there areas of your life where you are constantly comparing yourself to others? What are they and why?

5. What do you need to do right now to make Jesus' values the values of your Life Palette?

My One Priority regarding my values:

Action Plan:

Chapter Four

Through Squinted Eyes

It seems that nowadays we have an app for everything in life. There's an app to help us with our diets, to keep us on course with our exercise, and even to aid us in our spiritual journey.

I actually have an app on my phone called a "Value Viewer." It's designed for an artist, and will take any photo and reduce it down to its simple values for painting. It's a great tool. For the most part, though, I simply squint to see values because squinting allows me to better see the darks and the lights, the values that'll help me paint with more clarity. Perhaps you squint to help you focus on certain objects, like a highway sign.

However, I'm pretty sure squinting won't help you focus on the values you need on your Life Palette. And since there's no magic "Value Viewer" app to clearly define all your life's values, I want to show you a thought process that'll help you wrestle with your values. Yes, I mean wrestle: clarifying your values can be hard work, something only you can do. But you'll discover the benefit of having clarity for your values is amazing, and will add more worth to your life as the masterpiece God created you to be.

Ready for a "Do Over?"

Unless you carefully and prayerfully choose the values of your Life Palette, you become similar to a car ride at an amusement park. You've probably ridden one of them as a passenger. Your child or grandchild was driving and proudly steering, but not fully comprehending they weren't really in control at all. The small car's wheels, bumping from side to side on the track below, were guiding the car down the path. The steering wheel was only a prop.

Many people live like those amusement park cars, bumping from one direction to another, thinking that kind of life is as good as it gets, but wondering why they can never get off the path of frustration and misery. They never realize their values, or lack thereof, is a track forcing them down a road they would never have elected to travel in the first place. Regardless of what decisions are made, the road remains circular, always ending up back in the same spot. They give in to defeat and live what American author and poet Henry David Thoreau called "lives of quiet desperation."

> **You will never fully realize the dreams God has placed in your heart if you wait for the perfect circumstances.**

Perhaps you are existing with that same sense of hopelessness, or at least feel that it's true in some areas of your life. Still, the idea of being a masterpiece resonates with you—you secretly hope it to be true, want it to be true, and you've not quite given up hope altogether. It may just be that when it comes to the values on your Life Palette, you need a "do over."

When I was growing up on a farm in Ohio, there was a wooded pasture between my home and my grandparents' home that was my playground. During the summer months, my grandmother would mow a piece of that pasture to create a baseball diamond she lined out with lime. It looked like the real deal to a country farm boy, and even though I lived far from town, it was easy to get friends to come over to my house to play when I had my own personal baseball field. I felt like a king! The only thing that reminded us it was actually a pasture was the cow pies we avoided as we chased fly balls. It really wasn't all that bad; in fact, we often picked up a dry one and threw it in place of a baseball.

LIFE PALETTE

Chapter 5
Untouched
20 x 24"

Location: Grand Canyon National Park

From the artist: The colors, the rocks, the shadows, and the ever-changing weather make painting from the rim of the Grand Canyon fresh and new every time. Most people don't know the canyon for snow, yet winter in the canyon, when accessible, is stunning. The contrast of the snow reflecting the surrounding rocks and sky expand the Grand Canyon's abundant color palette. It is always challenging to paint, and equally rewarding.

Life Palette

Chapter 6

Solitary Repose
30 x 24"

Location: Old Marana, Arizona

From the artist: Every year in the desert, I look forward to the monsoon season. It is a time when we have thunderstorms and clouds build throughout the day on a fairly regular basis. The storms never last long, but they are usually severe and leave behind flash flooding. They always make for perfect sunsets. Kathy and I take advantage of monsoon season to go out into the desert as often as we can and watch the sunsets together and gather reference material for Arizona sunset compositions. *Solitary Repose* was painted in my studio from one of those moments when the sky near our home lit up with colors that only God could paint. Compared to the experience of this sunset, my attempt to capture His work on canvas is weak at best. Nevertheless, He gives me good material to work with every year during monsoons.

To view or purchase Jeff's art, check out www.jeffloveart.com

LIFE PALETTE

Chapter 7
Rock Climbers
18 x 24"
Location: Saguaro National Park West

From the artist: We live very close to the edge of Saguaro National Park West, so during the mild winters in Tucson I try to get in the park and paint *en plein air* on a regular basis. *Rock Climbers* is a painting that came about in my studio after one such outing. The saguaro cactus in the Sonoran desert is unique to our part of the world; they grow in the park like pine trees grow in a forest. They are, to say the least, intriguing, amazing beauty. I've painted them for years and still find them very captivating.

Chapter 8
Down Country Roads
15 x 28"

Location: Southeastern Utah

From the artist: I traveled with friend and artist Phil Starke on a painting trip through Utah. Before we left for the trip, another artist friend told us to watch for a particular road as we traveled through Utah and to be sure and get off the main road to paint it. We did just that, drove many miles down the road, and found several wonderful farms and ranches set in the southern Utah cliffs. For me, it's the best of both worlds. I love my roots growing up on a farm in Ohio and enjoy painting farms, and I love the west with its big skies and rock formations. If you are an artist and want to know the road, I will gladly share it with you. It's worth the journey.

When we played, if we didn't like the way we hit the ball—maybe it would slap a fresh cow pie, or strike a tree—we would simply yell "do over!" We got another chance at bat. It was as if the first hit never happened.

Now is that moment for you. It's time for a "do over." Maybe you've lived like a forgery up to this moment and succumbed to the idea this is all there is—and that you're not one of God's masterpieces. Perhaps you're at a new stage in life and need to reevaluate or go to a new level. Or it could simply be a good time for you to do a tune up to make sure you're giving God the very best values possible on your Life Palette.

The Lord wants you to be like a tree "planted along the riverbank, bearing fruit each season without fail. Their leaves never wither, and in all they do, they prosper." (Psalm 1:3) I'm drawn to paint trees by rivers, like in the painting in this book called "Glacier Bend," painted after a trip to Glacier National Park in Montana. Look at it…and take heart. Your second chance has arrived!

START WRESTLING

There are three simple questions you need to answer to bring clarity to your values, gain focus, and live with destiny. While the questions are simple in grammatical structure, they are by no means *simplistic*; however, taking the time now to wrestle with these questions will help to simplify your life in a very positive way. You'll face each day with vigor and enthusiasm you've never known before. Even more, you'll ensure your Life Palette is developed so God can create a masterpiece on the canvas of your life.

1. "What do I dream about?"

I'm not talking here of the fantasies my friends and I dreamed while playing on my homemade baseball diamond: bottom of the ninth in the World Series, bases loaded, and we knock it out of the park! The type of dream I'm talking about is far deeper—a passionate longing that's always been there but you just can't shake it. It's the kind of dream that haunts you; you want it so much it keeps you up at night. It's the dream you've whispered prayers about, hoping desperately God would answer with a "yes" or that He would miraculously change your life to sync up with your dream.

I knew a man who wanted more than anything to have a great marriage. He married a beautiful young woman in his early twenties. Not only was she lovely, but she was a woman of character. I sat in men's groups with this young man as he told the others about his perfect marriage, flawless children, and about all he did to make his wife and kids happy, serve them, and love them. Many times, men would come up to me privately after the meetings and confess they were jealous, wishing they could have his marriage and be as good a husband and father as he was.

His dream was to have a perfect marriage; unfortunately, his values didn't line up with his dream. At the same time he bragged about his perfect marriage, he was cheating on his wife with a younger woman. Eventually the marriage ended. The pain and confusion to his wife and children, not to mention his friends who thought things were perfect, was immeasurable. To have a "perfect" marriage or healthy relationship of any kind, you have to value it. Remember, it's not enough to *like* the idea of something; to value it, you have to *live* it.

From the prison to the palace

The Bible tells of a man who truly valued his dreams and lived them out, regardless of the cost. His name was Joseph, and his story is detailed in the last several chapters of Genesis. At the age of 17, God gave Joseph two specific dreams. First, he dreamed he and his brothers were working in a field tying up bundles of grain. His bundle stood up while all of his brother's bundles gathered around and bowed to his. In the second dream, the sun, moon, and 11 stars bowed before him.

They're not exactly dreams worth building your values on—unless you understand the deep, passionate desire God gave Joseph from the beginning: to be a leader. His dreams were images of his life being lived out with his family. Not surprisingly, Joseph's family was not exactly supportive of these dreams. "His brothers, responded, 'So you think you will be our king, do you? Do you actually think you will reign over us?' And they hated him all the more because of his dreams and the way he talked about them." (Genesis 37:8) In verse 10 Joseph's father, who favored him more than others, responded negatively as well: "'What kind of dream is that?' he asked. 'Will your mother and I and your brothers actually come and bow to the ground before you?'"

From the day Joseph knew the meaning of his dreams to the moment they were fulfilled; his life was full of drama. His brothers sold Joseph into slavery instead of killing him. He was in prison, out of prison, and back in again. Yet Joseph had God's dream for his life to be a leader, and it never wavered despite what others around him said or did, or regardless of the circumstances he was in. Joseph held tight to the dreams of his heart and built his values on them.

Once you determine your dream, it's vital you build your values on it. Otherwise the drama between knowing the dream and the fulfillment of the dream will derail you. How do you stay on track?

First, **be faithful in serving others** while waiting to see your dream become reality. Knowing you have a dream from God can make you believe others should just step aside and make a way for you. But Joseph understood while God had given him the dream, God also had a timeline that was known only to Him. Others weren't going to automatically accommodate it. It was going to take time. During the waiting, Joseph faithfully served others. "The LORD was with Joseph, so he succeeded in everything he did as he served in the home of his Egyptian

Between the Palette Scrapings with Phil Starke

As an artist, squinting helps simplify values and shapes. It helps you get rid of all the details that don't matter for a painting.

> **The natural result of living life as the masterpiece God created you to be is to bear joy.**

master. Potiphar noticed this and realized that the LORD was with Joseph, giving him success in everything he did. This pleased Potiphar, so he soon made Joseph his personal attendant. He put him in charge of his entire household and everything he owned...All his household affairs ran smoothly, and his crops and livestock flourished. So Potiphar gave Joseph complete administrative responsibility over everything he owned. With Joseph there, he didn't worry about a thing—except what kind of food to eat!" (Genesis 39:2-6) Because of his faithful service, God began to make Joseph's dream come true, even though it was probably not on the schedule Joseph had planned or in the way Joseph had imagined. When you have a dream, you often get sidetracked from serving faithfully in the present moment because you go in pursuit of something bigger. Yet it's God using you in your *present* circumstance which leads you to something bigger.

Second, **place others ahead of your agenda.** This requires you to be secure with who you are and what God created you to be. How you treat others when pursuing the dreams and passions God has given you is a reflection of how you think about yourself and how much you trust God. Jesus said this about greatness: "The greatest among you must be a servant. But those who exalt themselves will be humbled, and those who humble themselves will be exalted." (Matthew 23:11-12) God put Joseph in a position of leadership because of his faithful service while in prison, even though he was falsely accused. "Before long, the warden put Joseph in charge of all the other prisoners and over everything that happened in the prison. The warden had no more worries, because Joseph took care of everything. The LORD was with him and caused everything he did to succeed." (Genesis 39:22-23) By serving, Joseph was living his dream regardless of his circumstances.

Third, **continue to do the right things and see them as a training ground** preparing you for the fulfillment of your dream. Joseph went from the prison to the palace, ruling all of Egypt next to Pharaoh. Ultimately, his family did bow to him, but in a situation that reunited his family and saved their very lives. (Genesis 41-50) In the end, Joseph was able to say to his brothers, "You intended to harm me, but God intended it all for good. He brought me to this position so I could save the lives of many people." (Genesis 50:20)

You will never fully realize the dreams God has placed in your heart if you wait for the perfect circumstances to use the gifts God has given you. Joseph's dream wasn't realized by manipulation or self-promotion. He continued using his gifts and talents wherever God placed him. He never saw his circumstances as a dead end road to his God-inspired dream of leadership.

Dream big

Don't be afraid to let your dreams be "God sized." His dreams for you are big: they're His and they're significant. Don't dumb them down or try to reduce them to a level you know you can accomplish without Him. Instead, get the values on your Life Palette up to the plateau of the dream He has for you. Remember, your life as His masterpiece has more possibility that you can imagine. "Now all glory to God, who is able, through his mighty power at work within us, to accomplish infinitely more than we might ask or think." (Ephesians 3:20) The possibilities of what He can do in and through you are limitless, for "nothing is impossible with God." (Luke 1:37) You may feel like your situation is currently insurmountable for living the dream God has placed in your heart, but don't feel that way. Impossible thinking will keep you from discovering and living the values necessary on your Life Palette, and tie the hands of the artist as He paints your life as His masterpiece.

It's normal if you still have a hint of skepticism. You agree with the idea that nothing is impossible with God, but you interpret it to mean, "If He wants to." Living in the desert, I often see weather forecasts that predict a 30 percent chance of rain. Yet no one is taking their umbrellas with them that day. Why? Desert dwellers know it's possible it might rain, but not highly probable. Perhaps that's how you view God's "nothing is impossible" statement, so Jesus put it another way:

"Humanly speaking, it is impossible. But with God everything is possible." (Matthew 19:26) That perspective changes everything. Not only is it now possible, it's probable. That statement is a call to put faith into action when it comes to your values and your dreams.

How do you envision your life being lived? God will paint great relationships, great marriages, and great friendships on your life canvas, but only if the values on your Life Palette are the ingredients you know will allow you to serve others and place them ahead of you. Those values become the filter through which you make decisions. Will this job opportunity be best for my marriage? Will revealing something a friend told me in confidence make my friendship stronger or damage it? If you have a friend who has allowed addiction to take over his life, having healthy relationships as a value will allow you to confront and help him.

2. "What do I cry about?"

Here's where you consider what it is that God has given you a heart for—the thing that moves you to *compassion*.

When answering this question, be careful not to allow yourself to be manipulated by guilt. There are many noble causes that resort to using guilt to get you to buy into their vision. You've probably seen commercials on television that do this. The music is poignant, the pictures are compelling, and you feel a twinge of guilt rather than compassion. Suddenly you buy into the idea and it becomes one of your life values. You end up giving your money or time to the cause, only to discover that you quickly burn out. You receive a letter from them and you don't even want to open it. You're asked to give or serve again, and you look for any excuse to gracefully bow out. That is not something you "cry about." You're only being motivated by guilt.

Yet I have a friend who developed a ministry for pastors. If you were to ask him about his life, it would take just a few moments before he'd be telling you about pastors and their families because it's his passion and source of compassion. Broken marriages, divided parent-child relationships, burnout, even incidences of suicide are commonplace for those in church ministry. You may be shocked and even feel sad to the point you'd maybe whisper a prayer for your pastor. For my friend, though, this is something he cries about. God has given him such a burden for pastors that he has made it a value in his life. As a result, God is dipping into that value on his Life Palette and creating brush strokes on the canvas of his life—using him to encourage, help, and change the lives of pastors and their spouses and children.

Nehemiah is an ideal personalization of this value in the Bible. The city of Jerusalem was in ruins and unprotected. Nehemiah knew letting it remain that way would be a negative reflection on God's character to those who did not know Him. The plight of the city and the people made Nehemiah cry. "Hanani, one of my brothers, came to visit me with some other men who had just arrived from Judah. I asked them about the Jews who had returned there from captivity and about how things were going in Jerusalem. They said to me, 'Things are not going well for those who returned to the province of Judah. They are in great trouble and disgrace. The wall of Jerusalem has been torn down, and the gates have been destroyed by fire.' When I heard this, I sat down and wept. In fact, for days I mourned, fasted, and prayed to the God of heaven." (Nehemiah 1:2-4)

The destruction of the walls of Jerusalem moved Nehemiah very deeply. Up until this point, he was not a leader or a builder. There were likely plenty of people in a better position to do something about the problem. But God moved Nehemiah. The results were nothing short of miraculous. From this verse of tears to the completion of the wall, God opened one door after another, ultimately allowing Nehemiah to complete construction a mere 52 days after they began to rebuild. Nothing was impossible to Nehemiah!

Replacing guilt with compassion

It may seem complicated to discern the difference between compassion and guilt. However, you'll only get the correct core values on your Life Palette if you're directed by true compassion that God places in your heart. Here are three things to pray for as you ask the question, "What do I cry about"?

First, prayerfully **ask God to soften your heart.** You live in a world that encourages narcissism. To truly have the heart of compassion God wants for you, you must move beyond an "all about me" mentality.

When I was in college, I had a two-door sports car. It had a back seat, but you really couldn't get in and out of the car easily. It was more for show than for comfort or leg room. My wife Kathy and I kept that car for the first couple of years of our marriage as our only vehicle. Then one day, we discovered we were going to have a baby. It didn't take us long to realize our cute sports car wasn't going to work if we were going to have a family, so we traded it in for a four-door sedan that was practical and not nearly as sporty. It wasn't about us anymore, even with something as trite as a sports car.

As you ask God to soften your heart so you can experience His compassion, get ready. He will move you from self-centeredness to a place of maturity. Spiritually speaking, you will be trading in the sports car for the sedan. What's amazing is you're going to love it. I wouldn't trade the joy our children have brought us for all the sports cars in the world.

Second, **ask for God-given opportunities and the courage to meet them.** Compassion always demands action—and opportunities that move you with compassion will most likely be inconvenient and will cost you something. Consider the story of four men who were moved with compassion to get their paralyzed friend to Jesus so He could heal him. They carried him to the house where Jesus was teaching and found it to be packed with people. There was literally no room for them or their bed-ridden friend. However, their compassion was the real deal; they were moved beyond just a good idea. They knew they *had* to get him to Jesus, so they seized the opportunity God provided and were full of courage to act. "They dug a hole through the roof above his head. Then they lowered the man on his mat, right down in front of Jesus. Seeing their faith, Jesus said to the paralyzed man, 'My child, your sins are forgiven.'" (Mark 2:4-5)

Finally, **ask God to soften the hearts of those for whom He has given you compassion.** Never make the mistake of thinking you are obligated to force the compassion God has given you for someone or something onto others. God is the one who moves the hearts of others as you're faithful to act on the compassion He has placed within you. Give Him the space to do His work. Your job is to be certain about what you cry about so you can place the values on your Life Palette that align with that vision.

You may already know what makes you cry. Or perhaps you've known it for a long time but have never fully defined it. Take time to prayerfully wrestle with this question and you'll find a true, compelling passion that you'll want to have as a value on your Life Palette.

3. "What makes me laugh?"

"Wait a minute," you say. "You seriously expect me to base my values on what makes me laugh?" Don't underestimate the power of laughter, because this is all about *joy*, an important fruit—or visible evidence—of God's Spirit living in you. "But the Holy Spirit produces this kind of fruit in our lives: love, joy, peace, patience, kindness, goodness, faithfulness, gentleness, and self-control." (Galatians 5:22-23) Fruit is a natural result, not something forced or willed into existence.

My grandparents had grapevines on the farm where I grew up. Every year we had the expectation there would be grapes on the vine. I gladly helped pick them because I knew Grandma would take them and make homemade grape jelly. Yet I never saw Grandma go out and demand that the grapevines produce grapes (though that certainly would've made me laugh). They just did. It was the natural result of grapevines being grapevines.

The natural result of living life as the masterpiece God created you to be is to bear joy. "For the Kingdom of God is not a matter of what we eat or drink, but of living a life of goodness and peace and joy in the Holy Spirit." (Romans 14:17) Living in this joy will lead to living with power and ability, "for the joy of the LORD is your strength!" (Nehemiah 8:10) Yet the enemy of your soul is working overtime to cause you to live as a forgery by stealing your joy and steering you away from the fruit of the Spirit in you.

The Book of Joy

Paul wrote an entire letter about joy: the book of Philippians. He gives you some clear direction for keeping joy as a central part of your life and to keep the values on your Life Palette filled with joy!

In Philippians 3:1, Paul says, "Whatever happens, my dear brothers and sisters, rejoice in the Lord. I never get tired of telling you these things, and I do it to safeguard your faith." Seriously Paul…no matter what happens, rejoice? It helps to know Paul is writing this letter from prison, incarcerated for his faith and testimony, guilty only of being a follower of Jesus. He was facing a possible execution when he wrote those words. Maybe you've felt your circumstances are pressing in on you so heavily, you can't go any further. How do you continue? Joy. Know what brings you the greatest joy and keep living in the fruit of the Spirit, regardless of your circumstances. How? By trusting Him completely in difficulty, and by living in faith that God is in control even when you're under intense trial or experiencing overwhelming sorrow.

Between the Palette Scrapings with Phil Starke

In painting, as in life, it helps to simplify values. There are more values in nature than an artist can paint. I try to narrow down to three values. When I get over four or five values, it becomes too complicated to paint.

A great way to live in joy is to look for the best in others. "Some are preaching out of jealousy and rivalry…They preach with selfish ambition, not sincerely, intending to make my chains more painful to me. But that doesn't matter. Whether their motives are false or genuine, the message about Christ is being preached either way, so I rejoice. And I will continue to rejoice." (Philippians 1:15-18) Paul admitted their motives were impure, yet he was looking for the best in them and continuing to rejoice and live in joy. The alternative is to allow others to steal your joy and actually control how you feel. That'll negatively affect what's placed on your Life Palette.

So how do you do this when others hurt you? The key is to have the same outlook toward others that Jesus possessed. "Don't be selfish; don't try to impress others. Be humble, thinking of others as better than yourselves. Don't look out only for your own interests, but take an interest in others, too. You must have the same attitude that Christ Jesus had." (Philippians 2:3-5) Look at others knowing God has created them as His masterpiece, same as He did you. He's given them gifts, talents, and a destiny to honor Him just as He has given those things to you.

> **Nothing will simplify your life more and empower you greater than to know when to say "Yes" and "No."**

In Philippians 4:10-12, Paul shares a third secret to living in joy. "How I praise the Lord...for I have learned how to be content with whatever I have. I know how to live on almost nothing or with everything. I have learned the secret of living in every situation, whether it is with a full stomach or empty, with plenty or little." Contentment is never an outward thing; it always comes from the joy of the Lord. You may be in the middle of some of the worst experiences in your life, yet you can experience joy through being content. Joy leads to values on your Life Palette that'll help you live as His masterpiece.

Finally, Paul encourages you to refocus your thoughts: "Don't worry about anything; instead, pray about everything. Tell God what you need, and thank him for all he has done." (Philippians 4:6) Through Him, the one who created you as a masterpiece, you can have a joy not found anywhere else or through anyone else. Worry will rob you of joy and steal your peace of mind. Worry is a sign you do not trust God or His ability to act on His promises on your behalf. These are values that will hinder your Life Palette. If you've prayed about something and are continuing to pray about something, why worry? God is not panicked or anxious and He certainly doesn't want worry to be on your Life Palette. He wants joy! Refocus as you "fix your thoughts on what is true, and honorable, and right, and pure, and lovely, and admirable. Think about things that are excellent and worthy of praise." (Philippians 4:8)

My friend who cries because of his ministry for pastors will tell you that seeing them receive help and freedom brings him the greatest joy. He'd also tell you that he stays awake at night thinking about how to help them. The fact that the answers to all three questions align in the way these values are lived out in his life affirms he is fulfilling the destiny God has for him. As you wrestle with these questions, you'll identify similar passions in your life—and discover your destiny as God's masterpiece.

COUNTER THE CRITICS

Be warned. Once you have clearly defined the values on your Life Palette, others—friends, loved ones, even Satan himself—will heat up the battle to tempt you to go against them. There are many reasons why they want to see you go back to living life like the amusement car ride, bumping along and ending up back in the same spot. It may be they see you headed in a direction they never had the courage to take themselves. It may be they truly think they know what's best for you. Remember, God is the artist. He is the one leading you to develop the values necessary on your Life Palette for a masterpiece. Whatever the reason someone may have for wanting to keep you where you are, that's not what God has planned for you.

Plus, consider the benefits of living out your core life values. Nothing will simplify your life more and empower you greater than to know when to say "Yes" and "No." Your core life values will give you a *standard* for all your decisions; they become the filter that'll keep you on course and from making choices that can destroy your life as God's masterpiece. Ask God for strength, power, and courage to live the values He's led you to live. Prayerfully ask Him for wisdom and direction.

For an artist working on creating a masterpiece, values are critical. He knows if the values are right, the rest of the painting will be right.

Each brush stoke of color that brings the painting to life is relative to the values. Yet once the values are right, the artist must take another thing into consideration for his palette, as you must for your Life Palette. It's called composition: highly debatable, hard to define, but endlessly fascinating to explore and vital to master.

Palette Points

1. What do you dream about? In other words, what do you see that *could be* and *should be*?

2. What do you cry about? What breaks your heart and stirs righteous anger within you? How does it impact you emotionally and spiritually?

3. What do you laugh about? What gives you the greatest joy in life?

4. Are you able to see a common thread through what you dream about, cry about, and laugh about? How does that point toward core values for your Life Palette?

5. What keeps you from taking action on your core values? What do you need to do to remove these barriers?

My One Priority regarding my core values:

Action Plan:

Chapter Five

Good, Bad or U-g-l-y

When it's good, it paves the way for a potential masterpiece. When it's bad, it undermines every effort an artist exerts in creating a masterpiece. When it's ugly, well, you know the saying: it's just "U-G-L-Y, you ain't got no alibi…"

What is it? It's composition. In the art world, there's probably nothing more debatable or difficult than a good composition. Composition itself is simple to define; it's the arrangement of shapes and the balancing of elements to form the whole. However, it's hard to go much beyond that and still find agreement. Most artists believe they are able to recognize a good composition, especially when they're the ones creating it on their canvas. Yet when it comes to compositions created by their peers, they question the choices made and disagree about what really makes a good composition.

There is a difference between composition and design, yet the two are often referred to as one and the same among many artists. Clarity of the two, though, is important for the development of your Life Palette. One refers to the bigger picture of your life in relationship to God as your Creator having a destiny and plan for your life; the other has to do with what you do with it and how you limit or empower Him.

Design is creating something from nothing, whereas composition is taking elements that already exist and arranging them for what the artist feels is a balanced picture. God alone is the designer of your life. He's the one who has created something from nothing and has given you a good, pleasing and hopeful destiny.

Life Palette

The designer

It's important to nail down *who* is the designer of your life in order to fully understand how your Life Palette affects the composition of your life. Many would argue they are the designers of their own lives, are in complete control, and that God has nothing to do with their destiny and future. Should the composition of their lives represent a masterpiece, they alone should receive the credit. Interestingly, should their lives turn out to be a forgery, they equally believe someone else should get the blame—be it God, parents, or even the government.

What's freeing for you to understand is that it's the *artist alone* who makes the decisions regarding composition. Since we have concluded that God is the artist for our lives, we then know He is in control of the composition: He is working to form the whole of our lives as His masterpiece, arranging the shapes and balancing the elements as only He can. But, as the artist of our lives, God is also either *empowered or limited* by what we choose to place on our Life Palette.

There are many decisions an artist makes to create a great composition: the size of different shapes, the placement of them, and the determination of the focal point. Some of the questions an artist will ask before creating a composition are, "What do I want to do with the subject?" "What is the desired end result?" "What am I trying to express?" A great artist never just puts something in a composition simply because "it's there." They have a reason. It's all a part of their plan to create a masterpiece. Every decision made regarding composition is a reflection of the artist's personality and desires.

As an artist, one of the things I hate is when someone sees a painting I'm working on and comments about it. I totally understand why they do it; things just don't look right to them. Even though they're not artists, they inherently know enough about composition—because they have seen God's masterful compositions in nature—to feel they know enough to express their opinion. What they don't know, however, is what I have in mind for the finished painting, and what's necessary to go through first to get to the end result. Another artist will see the same piece and give comments from an understanding of this process. They will say things like, "Tell me where you are going with this piece."

If God is the artist and I am the masterpiece, I need to trust He is using all things toward the end result of His desire, for "we know that God causes everything to work together for the good of those who love God and are called according to his purpose for them." (Romans 8:28) Yet you may be thinking, "Well, if God is the artist who is automatically working everything to fulfill His purpose, then what part do I have regarding the composition of my life?" There are several things that are of *your choosing* on your Life Palette that you give God to work with: character, priorities, choices, focus, and simplicity. These things are to your life what composition is to painting. The more clearly you align these areas with God's Word, the more He is able to compose your life according to His plan and design.

Between the Palette Scrapings with Phil Starke

Painting is about deciding what's important and what's not. You can't paint it all. You must prioritize what to leave out and what to put in.

GOD'S INVISIBLE QUALITIES

Lest you're concerned God is incapable of creating a composition for your life that would lead to masterpiece living, or feel you may be able to do better on your own, just look at nature. It's understandable why the compositions found in nature are masterpieces when we grasp the fact that nature reflects the artist, God. In Romans 1:19-20, Paul says people "know the truth about God because he has made it obvious to them. For ever since the world was created, people have seen the earth and sky. Through everything God made, they can clearly see his invisible qualities—his eternal power and divine nature. So they have no excuse for not knowing God." The composition of nature reflects the invisible qualities of God in the same way we are His creation, His masterpiece, and reflect His invisible qualities. Paul says that in the composition of nature, God's invisible qualities are "clearly" seen. They cannot be missed or misunderstood.

My painting "Untouched" is one of the many compositions I've painted of the Grand Canyon. I'll never forget the first time I saw the canyon. I was blown away! Before that moment, I had friends describe it to me and I had seen pictures, but neither had done it justice. It's absolutely awe-inspiring. As I stood on the rim for the first time, I was reminded of Romans 1:19-20. Everything about its incredible composition reflects the invisible qualities of God. I could almost imagine Him carving that masterpiece with His fingertips. The psalmist expressed that same feeling when he wrote Psalm 8:3-4: "When I look at the night sky and see the work of your fingers—the moon and the stars you set in place—what are mere mortals that you should think about them, human beings that you should care for them?" The psalmist understood completely that the masterpiece compositions found in creation reflect its Creator.

> **Character is not a thing you do; rather, it is developed in you through faithful endurance.**

In the same way, if you were to see a painting that's considered a masterpiece, you would conclude things about the artist. If it were a nice pastoral country landscape, you would assume they love the country and nature. Were the painting of a New York City street bustling with people and cars, you could safely assume they are drawn to the excitement of city life. Regardless of the subject matter and all you may draw from it, it's safe to assume the artist of any masterpiece is a person of intelligence and talent, and through their masterpiece you see their personality and qualities revealed. You'd never wonder how a blank canvas sitting in a studio was somehow covered with paint and turned into a wonderful composition on its own. Clearly the paint did not leap from the tube so that a masterpiece came into existence. Rather, through the artist's design, careful planning, and labor, a compositional masterpiece is created.

Composition and character

I started out in ministry as a youth pastor and worship leader. As a young man, my passion was art and music, so I was thrilled when my wife Kathy and I received an invitation from a church in Hereford, Texas to serve as their worship pastor. Hereford was a big change for us geographically, coming from the farms of Ohio and finishing high school in Colorado. Living in west Texas was a shocker. It's flat terrain suggested that during creation God took His hand and scraped everything west of the Mississippi and piled it up to create the Rockies. Needless to say, we missed the mountains, but we loved the people of West Texas.

One of the couples dear to Kathy and I was John David and Bev. They took us in as their own and poured love and life into us. We had mutual interest not only in our church, but also in our passion for antiques. Their home was a collector's dream house. Early on, John David invited me to join him on a Saturday morning at an old building downtown. It was scheduled to be remodeled and he was going to tear out the old tin ceiling before the other interior work was started. John David worked out a deal to keep the tin pieces he removed, and he offered to give me some of the pieces if I helped him finish the work.

We began kicking the tins off of the rafters from the top down. Several times one hard kick would leave us hanging perilously from the 12 foot ceiling. Most people would have let pros do this type of demolition work. It was dusty and sweaty and painful. By midday, we had kicked down every tin and loaded them for storage. We divided the booty (I later used my portion for some great wall design) and as we wrapped up, John David looked at me. "You know," he said, "the real reason I invited you to help me today is I wanted to see what you were made of." John David was talking about character.

Paul gives us insight into character in Romans 5:3-5. "We can rejoice, too, when we run into problems and trials, for we know that they help us develop endurance. And endurance develops strength of character, and character strengthens our confident hope of salvation. And this hope will not lead to disappointment. For we know how dearly God loves us, because he has given us the Holy Spirit to fill our hearts with his love."

I want to be known as a man of character. More specifically, when people check to see what I'm made of, I want them to see the character of Christ. But I'm not so fond of the way Paul connects the dots between character, problems and trials, and endurance. There has to be a short cut to having character, right? Wrong! My grandmother used to say the longest distance between two points is a shortcut. There are no shortcuts to character.

What you are "made of" is imperative for living life as the masterpiece God created you to be. However, character is not a thing you do; rather, it is developed in you through faithful endurance. It seems somewhat demented when Paul says, "We can rejoice, too, when we run into problems and trials." That's normally not my first reaction to difficulty. Yet what could possibly make you want to praise God when you face a problem? The confident knowledge that God is working on a masterpiece. It's your trust that the artist has a design that'll lead to a composition which will ultimately reflect His qualities.

I've gone through many things in my life, especially in ministry, that given the choice I would never go through again. While I don't want to repeatedly endure painful trials, I'm so grateful for what God teaches me through them, and for how He gives me the strength to persevere and allow my character to be strengthened. The word "character" in Romans 5:4 comes from the Greek word *dokime*, which communicates the concept of being proved by trial. It's like John David inviting me to help tear down a ceiling to see what I'm made of. Both of us saw evidence of my resolve and were each strengthened as a result.

Three keys to character development

Since character is such an important addition to your Life Palette, what are some choices you can make to help God develop His character within you? In the Old Testament, God gave Jeremiah a great illustration from the art world so Israel could learn about character development—one we can still learn from today. "The LORD gave another message to Jeremiah. He said, 'Go down to the potter's shop, and I will speak to you there.' So I did as he told me and found the potter working at his wheel. But the jar he was making did not turn out as he had hoped, so he crushed it into a lump of clay again and started over. Then the LORD gave me this message: 'O Israel, can I not do to you as this potter has done to his clay? As the clay is in the potter's hand, so are you in my hand.'" (Jeremiah 18:1-6)

Artists today still throw clay on a wheel much as they did in Jeremiah's day. The potter's wheel has been modernized by technology: I would choose today's motorized wheel any day over one that I would have to kick to turn. But the concept of creating a piece of pottery is still the same today, and there are three things we can learn about character development from the creative visual God gave Jeremiah.

1. Be pliable

If you've ever watched a potter working clay on a wheel, you've seen the importance of pliable clay. In order for the potter to compose the clay into the masterpiece he has in mind, the clay needs to remain supple, and able to bend without breaking. The more pliable the clay, the more it responds to every move of the potters hand, to every touch of his fingers as he creates and designs. As the clay hardens and becomes less pliable, the potter has to work with greater force and effort.

The picture of the potter crushing the clay to start over is significant. It's not that the potter is angry or venting his frustrations on the clay. It's that the potter as the artist has a masterpiece in mind and is working to shape the clay into that masterpiece, but it has hardened and he's no longer able to work with it. The more pliable we remain, the more God can shape our character.

We can so easily get set in our ways, especially as we grow older and become more accustomed to the routine of daily life. Yet when you see what God is doing in the lives of your friends or someone at church, ask yourself how you would respond if God wanted to work in your life that same way. If you respond, "No way!" or "That'll take me way out of my comfort zone," you may need to ask Him to help you be pliable. There may be a lot He wants to develop in your character, but you are hardening your heart to His work within you. Remember, character development is not about God being mean, cruelly wanting to see how much you can endure. In truth, He already knows how much you can endure. It's all about Him needing you to see what you are made of.

2. Be receptive

The potter starts over because the molding of the clay did not turn out right the first time. Imagine the clay then saying, "Uh-uh. I may not be the masterpiece you created me to be, but I'm good enough as is. Just leave me alone." The clay would never become the far greater masterpiece it was intended to be.

Most of us live our lives far beneath the privilege God has for us because we are not receptive to how He is working to develop our character. We live as forgeries, cheap imitations, and often whine and complain to Him about it. To remain receptive, we must tune into what God is doing in our lives each day, and stay in constant communication with Him through prayer and reading His Word, the Bible.

3. Be grateful

You will never hear a piece of pottery verbally speak to the artist after it has been completed and say "thank you." The pottery has no choice but to reflect the handiwork of the artist and therefore reflect it, so to speak, with gratefulness. We have a choice. We can live our entire lives with ingratitude to the artist of our lives. How much more, though, will God work with us as His masterpiece when we respond to Him with grateful hearts!

Gratefulness is a trust issue. Do you really believe God is working on your character to create a masterpiece? If you've ever played sports, you've probably had the experience of a coach pushing you beyond what you considered your limit. You didn't like it and it may have even made you mad. Yet as your skill reached new heights, you were appreciative for the coach seeing something in you that you couldn't see in yourself.

God sees more in you than you could possibly see in yourself—and He is working to develop you so He can continue creating a masterpiece. Paul said you *can* rejoice when you run into troubles and trials because God is working toward an end result. You choose whether or not to rejoice and be grateful for all God is doing. An ungrateful heart may cause you to miss all that He is doing to develop your character. That would be unfortunate.

Character Indicators

I'm not sure about how all things work in heaven, especially right after we die. I often imagine that I'll be able to peer in on my own funeral as the proverbial fly on the wall. I probably won't care about anything earthly at that point. All the questions I have for God will more than likely be irrelevant since I'll have a true eternal perspective for the first time. But I want to hear what my wife, kids, and friends have to say about me after I'm gone. The sum total of one's character is revealed most in the words of those who are saying good-bye to you for the last time on this earth. I'd hate to realize at that moment that I'd been on the wrong path with my character and that it had hindered God in painting a masterpiece with my life.

Most of us live our lives far beneath the privilege God has for us.

The good news is there are indicators along the way that reveal whether we are taking the right character path or the wrong one. One of those indicators is what those closest to you are saying now about your character. It's possible those same people will be speaking at your funeral, or at the very least attending and conversing with others about you. Listen with a discerning heart. If for whatever reason you can't hear what they are saying, set aside some time to seek their honest feedback. Ask them to describe what they think you are made of.

We've all heard the saying, "When the going gets tough, the tough get going." That's trite but true. Perhaps more suited for our conversation is, "When the going gets tough, those with a well-developed character get going (and those who are in need of serious character development quit)." In Romans 5:4, Paul reveals the importance of endurance, which "develops strength of character, and character strengthens our confident hope of salvation." Being on the right path with character will always lead to hope that God will see you through—and that ultimately He, as the artist of your life, has everything in control as He paints your life into the portrait that looks much like His son Jesus: "Just as we are now like the earthly man, we will someday be like the heavenly man." (1 Corinthians 15:49) After all, God cares much more about the finished product as a masterpiece than simply delivering us from a momentary problem or trial. All that we see in Jesus and His character is a glimpse of the masterpiece God has in mind for our future. The more we get to know Him, the more we understand Him and His character. The more we become like Him, the more we will live as the masterpiece He created us to be.

The most important thing we can do to assure we are on the right path with our character is to model our lives after the character of Jesus. Paul tells us in Galatians 3:27 to "put on" the character of Christ. We see the character of Jesus as we read in the Bible about His life here on earth. He endured problems and trials most of us will never come close to experiencing. We also see His character traits identified in Galatians 5:22-23: "But the Holy Spirit produces this kind of fruit in our lives: love, joy, peace, patience, kindness, goodness, faithfulness, gentleness, and self-control."

COMPOSITION AND PRIORITIES

In his novel *The Mysterious Island*, author Jules Verne writes about five men who hijack a balloon to escape from prison. It rose in the air and the wind soon blew it out over the ocean, but as the journey continued the balloon began to lose altitude. The men soon realized they were going to crash into the surface of the ocean and possibly drown unless they discarded some weight from the basket of their balloon. They began by tossing out the non-essentials; shoes, weapons, coats, and the balloon rose once again, but only temporarily. As they sank toward the water once again, they had to lose more weight. They concluded it was better to continue in the air hungry than to drown, so they threw their food overboard and, ultimately, even their gold. Still, the balloon continued to descend, so they decided to cut the ropes holding the very basket they were standing in, leaving them clinging to the meshes. The balloon rose and they survived until they finally spotted land.

Those men were taught a lesson about priorities we'd do well to learn. As long as the gas in the balloon kept them at a comfortable altitude, they kept things in the basket that seemed essential to them. Yet they quickly realized their true priorities as they sank toward certain death in the ocean. What they thought was essential became trivial and was quickly discarded.

Priorities affect the composition of your life. The shapes and pieces God is working with are a direct result of your priority choices on your Life Palette. In Romans 6:16, Paul tells you why this is so critical to your life's composition: "Don't you realize that you become the slave of whatever you choose to obey? You can be a slave to sin, which leads to death, or you can choose to obey God, which leads to righteous living."

A person's priorities are clearly seen not by what they say they want to achieve, but what they actually do. For instance, if a person says their marriage is a priority in their life and they love their spouse but have an extramarital affair once a year, then it's clear that having a healthy marriage is not a true priority.

Determining your priorities

While I'm not going to give you a list of priorities for your life, I do want to give you a starting point that will help you focus or realign your priorities on your Life Palette. Paul shows you where to begin when he says, "This is the secret: Christ lives in you…" (Colossians 1:27) That's the basis for a great life composition. The next step is to spend time prayerfully considering what priorities God would have you set. James 1:5 says, "If you need wisdom, ask our generous God, and he will give it to you. He will not rebuke you for asking." God wants to instruct you in your priorities. He is the ultimate source of guidance and He has revealed Himself clearly through His Word. Confirm what you sense through prayer by comparing it with the Bible. He will never go against Scripture.

> **God sees more in you than you could possibly see in yourself.**

I can't tell you how many times as a pastor I've had someone tell me they are considering leaving their spouse because they've found someone else and ask me to join them in prayer. Amazingly, they're stunned when I tell them I won't pray for them and that, frankly, they can quit praying themselves about it because God has already made Himself very clear about the sanctity of marriage. So as you are seeking God for His priorities for your Life Palette, know what He has already revealed in His Word. "So be careful how you live. Don't live like fools, but like those who are wise." (Ephesians 5:15) The New King James version of that verse says to "walk circumspectly."

You should also seek wise counsel from others as you seek His priorities for your Life Palette, but be warned: wise counsel only comes from wise people. It's dangerous to seek the counsel of someone who will just agree with you. Often the best advice is contrary to your own desires. The apostle Paul himself sought the wise counsel of the other disciples in Acts 9 after spending three years praying and preparing for ministry.

Finally, ask God to help you drill down your priorities to only a few. We live in a day and time where we celebrate multitasking and think we can do it all. I find it interesting that the person who is usually trying to do way too much is usually the one trying to convince me they're great at multitasking. Typically, we are not as good at it as we think we are and the results prove it. We end up being mediocre at many things. As my dad used to say, "Jack of all trades, master of none."

You win or lose by the way you choose

One of the things I love about the approach of each New Year is how everyone stops to consider their priorities and how they intend to live them out in the coming 12 months. As a pastor I try to take advantage of that season with a teaching that will help people make true life-changing commitments. The unfortunate part of New Year's ponderings is that it comes but once a year. We tend to overlook the power of *daily* choices regarding our priorities. We underestimate the importance of what we do each day and overestimate the importance of what we do in a week or a month or a year. The sad result is that we often squander our days waiting for some big moment to move us. The success of living our priorities on our Life Palette is found in our daily choices. We win or lose each day by the way we choose.

This centers around two things God uses to paint our lives as a masterpiece: decisions and discipline. Each is very different. Many people make a New Year's resolution to lose weight—a decision. However, when asked if they are making plans to give up their favorite food or dessert, they're not quite ready to do that. They lack discipline.

There is incredible power in a simple decision, but it must be in line with the priorities of your Life Palette. Most people grossly underestimate the cost of making a decision that goes against a priority. Discipline, too, is an incredible gift God has given you to help you succeed, but following through on the daily disciplines necessary to live out the priorities of your Life Palette is not easy.

In my early twenties I was leading music at a weeklong youth camp. An extremely creative person, I always struggled with discipline. I didn't like routine or deadlines. I wanted everything to be fresh and new. That week was life changing for me. I don't remember the lady's name who was the main speaker, but she pulled me aside one day, looked me in the eyes, and said, "Jeff, God has given you a great talent of creativity, but unless you learn some discipline, He will never be able to use you." I use to think God gave her great discernment, but looking back I think everyone who knew me could see it; she was just the first one to have the guts to tell me. And she was right. To this day, I'm still not the most disciplined person I know, but I have learned to look at discipline as a friend, a tool God has blessed me with that, used wisely, will allow Him to create a wonderful composition for my life.

Organize or Agonize

God is a God of organization. It doesn't take much research to see and understand this truth. Just look at our solar system. God is a God of systems. Without a good system in any area of our lives, we agonize. Notice I said *good* system, because we do everything by systems, both good and bad.

Between the Palette Scrapings with Phil Starke

Good composition goes a long way towards making a painting work. Even with lack of color or technique, a good composition can still be interesting, likable, and strong. However, a bad composition will ruin good color and the best of technique.

I have a Golden Retriever named Hubble. He's a big dog, weighing about 90 pounds. When Hubble was about one year old, he would get up in one of the lounge chairs on the back porch. While he loved being up in the chair, he was afraid to get down. When Hubble decided it was time to get out of the chair, he would bark until one of us went out and grabbed him by the collar. We didn't have to pull him down;

he just needed the assurance we were there. He may have thought we were helping him down, but we weren't and he certainly didn't need us to assist. He was plenty capable.

One day I had settled down on the couch and, sure enough, Hubble started barking. I did what I normally did and called for one of the kids to go out and help him down. No one heard me. Hubble continued barking, and I continued calling to no avail. I realized in that moment that the dog and my family had a system in place. Hubble would get on his chair, he would bark, and one of us would go out and make him feel as if we were helping him down. It was a system that was no longer delivering the results I desired, so I decided I was going to introduce Hubble to a new system. I got some of his favorite food and went outside. This time, instead of touching him and making him think I was assisting him, I put the food on the porch in front of him. He continued barking, but I kept telling him that he could get down, bribing him with the tasty treat. Slowly, he put his paw on the ground and, with great trepidation, stepped off his chair. Over the next several days I moved his chair inside so we could keep working with Hubble to remind him he could get down off his chair by himself. Soon, the new system was working like a charm. Again, it wasn't that Hubble wasn't capable; but when he was a small pup I had put a system in place that Hubble thought he had to operate by in order to get down.

Our lives revolve around systems. God designed it that way. It's so important we are intentional with the systems we use. The key is to initiate. In what areas of your life are you allowing a bad system—the way you do something—to hinder your Life Palette? A poor system for any area of your life will result in you agonizing over it. The more organized you are, the more you empower God to balance the composition of your life.

I'll never forget the moment in high school after I'd been told I had a lead role in a musical. A girl who tried out for the part told me I was always so lucky and expressed her disdain because she never got the parts she wanted. I asked if she practiced singing, and she said "no." I asked if she'd taken lessons, and she said "no." I asked her how many hours she worked on the songs in the musical before the tryouts, and she said she hadn't worked on them more than a few minutes. What she didn't understand was that it wasn't luck. I'd taken lessons and spent many lonely hours of rehearsal. I certainly wasn't the most naturally talented person, but I'd learned to work within an organized system in that area of my life.

Keeping your priorities in place

Trophies are not handed out at the beginning of a race. They come at the finish line. Finishing the race is a result of living by your priorities every day. Paul said in 2 Timothy 4:7: "I have fought the good fight, I have finished the race, and I have remained faithful." One of the tools for helping you finish the race is to keep your priorities in place—and live by them every day. At the end of each day, ask yourself, "How did I do in living out the priorities that I've prayerfully determined?" Make a decision to eliminate anything that goes against your priorities. Be brutal. You must work daily on your Life Palette to assure you live according to the priorities God has set before you. When you are tired and weary, remember the trophy at the finish line: a masterpiece. His masterpiece.

Leonardo da Vinci is noted for saying, "Paintings are never finished; they're just abandoned." Fortunately, da Vinci is not the artist of your life. God will finish the good work He has begun composing on the canvas of your life. He will never abandon you.

The better these foundational truths of your Life Palette are understood and lived, the greater is your potential to live as the masterpiece God created you to be. But everyone knows that one thing that attracts people to a painting they like is color. You may like brilliant colors that make you feel alive, or colors that calm your spirit and give you a sense of peace. Getting the priorities of your Life Palette in order allows you to begin adding the colors to your Life Palette that make your life exciting.

Palette Points

1. Are you pliable, receptive, and grateful, allowing God to work on your character as His masterpiece? Are there any of these three areas where you need to make a change on your Life Palette? What are they, and what changes do you need to make right now?

2. List your top five priorities and describe why each of them is a priority on your Life Palette. What do you need to do to make your relationship with God the number one priority on your Life Palette?

3. How are your daily choices helping or hurting you in living out your priorities? What new choices do you need to make to live your priorities on your Life Palette?

4. Consider how you systematically go about living your life each day. What are the results you are achieving? How can you change how you systematically live to get the results you desire (and God wants) in your life as His masterpiece?

My One Priority regarding character, priorities and choices on my Life Palette:

Action Plan:

Chapter 9
Fearless
24 x 36"

Location: Oak Creek Canyon, Sedona, Arizona

From the artist: There are few places as unique and beautiful as Sedona, Arizona. Living as close as we do, we plan regular painting trips to the Red Rock country. *Fearless* is a painting that came about from a reference picture my wife first took on our way to Oak Creek Canyon. I had taken the reference with me to a workshop with Matt Smith and painted a small study in the workshop. Since then, I have traveled back to this spot and have painted a variety of compositions of this precarious rock in my studio. This painting appeared in Southwest Art magazine, April 2012, and was chosen to represent the Arizona Plein Air Painters.

Chapter 10
Rising Tide
36 x 36"

Location: Heceta Beach, Oregon coast

From the artist: We spent our honeymoon at a resort not far from Heceta beach in Oregon many years ago. Since then, we have made many trips to the coast to visit family and to paint. Heceta beach is a popular area close to Florence, Oregon, and is most known for the lighthouse that stands guard on the cliffs overlooking the beach. It is a place we typically visit on trips to see our family. While the lighthouse is beautiful and worth the visit, the landscape of the Pacific Ocean crashing into the coast and continually carving out its signature draws me to paint it and try to capture its awe-inspiring beauty.

To view or purchase Jeff's art, check out www.jeffloveart.com

Chapter 11

Arroyo Rosa
24 x 36"
Location: Old Marana, Arizona

From the artist: *Arroyo Rosa* was another one of the breathtaking sunsets we've come to expect during our monsoon season. This piece was chosen for the Empire "100" Western Art Show and Sale. It is a show I have been privileged to be a part of for several years. It raises funds for the preservation of the historic Empire Ranch Headquarters, a famous old western ranch near Sonoita, Arizona. Each fall they do a big roundup: fun to visit and to paint the ranch.

Chapter 12

Isn't She Lovely
16 x 20"
Location: Mt. Moran, Grand Teton National Park
From the artist: Mt. Moran is my favorite peak in the Grand Tetons, not only for its remarkable beauty, but for its namesake as well. Thomas Moran was an American painter and printmaker from the Hudson River School in New York. His paintings would often feature the Rocky Mountains. His work played an important role in the creation of Yellowstone National Park. He paved the way for all of us today who love to travel and paint the national parks. Mt. Moran is one of those places I have painted many times and plan to paint many more times in the future. I have a friend who had a client who owned a painting hanging in her room, passed down through the family. They were all shocked to discover it was an original Thomas Moran.

Chapter Six

Color Harmony

If you were to research how many colors the human eye can perceive, you'd quickly discover the number to be astounding—as many as 20 million. God, the Creator of the universe—and all colors—was prolific in this area. On a smaller scale, my latest check of a website of my favorite brand of oil paints revealed over 100 different tubes of color to choose from.

An artist may get the values perfect and have a composition that's sure to be a masterpiece, but without the beautiful variety of color, the attraction of a painting for the viewer will be lost. Color is one of the most powerful tools an artist has to influence the person looking at their painting. Color is the thing that compels many artists to paint in the first place. With color, the artist can establish depth: giving the viewer a three-dimensional sense as they look at a one-dimensional canvas surface. With color, the artist creates the mood: bright reds and yellows give a sense of vibrancy and life, while a painting full of grays may create an atmosphere that feels gloomy and sad. For the artist, the possibilities are endless. Each color choice heightens the emotional impact they wish to convey. As you can see from my painting "Solitary Repose," I love color. While there is a great variety of color in a beautiful Arizona sunset like this one, it is a great example of color harmony, each one affecting the other.

While the options with color are never-ending, so are the decisions. One of the most confusing choices for a beginning artist is which colors of paint to put on their palette. With all of its allure, color is one of the greatest challenges for an artist because there are so many colors to consider.

Life Palette

Color is to painting what relationships are to life

One of the greatest problems we face in creating our Life Palette is relationships. Like color, relationships give life depth and dimension, energy and vibrancy, emotional strength and stability. Relationships are a necessary and natural part of life. They are also one of the most powerful and valuable assets affecting our Life Palette. Relationships make all the difference between lives lived as a masterpiece or as a forgery.

Every relationship you have has an impact on your Life Palette, as well as how God the master artist ultimately paints the daily brush strokes on your life canvas. Some add tremendous value, always encouraging you to go to new heights, while others have a negative effect and, left unattended, could keep you from your destiny. The apostle Paul says it this way in 1 Corinthians 15:33: "Bad company corrupts good character."

Of course, while we get to choose some of our relationships (our spouse and most friends, for example), we don't get to select all of them. We didn't choose our parents, our siblings, our co-workers, or the neighbor who moved in next door. Even if we had that privilege, with our limited knowledge of the future we'd probably still make wrong choices. Just take a look at couples who marry and later divorce. At one point, they couldn't live without each other. They thought the other person added so much value to their life they wanted to spend the rest of their life with them. If we were comparing their relationship in those early stages to a painting, they would have described it as the vivid reds that gave vibrancy to their life, the beautiful yellows that illuminated every day like a summer sun. In the end, however, it turned gray and dark.

To assure relationships add value to your Life Palette, it's important to forever grow in your understanding of how to relate to others. On the surface, you may think that sounds silly; after all, you're already relating to your family, coworkers, and neighbors. However, unless you choose to develop your relationships, they will soon grow stale and become a detriment to the success of your life, and theirs. This is not God's intent. As you continue to develop your relational skills, you can and should add value to the people you know and love, and to all the others who cross your path until the day you die.

Color Harmony

Between the Palette Scrapings with Phil Starke

Using a color that is discordant will throw off the color harmony of the entire painting. Color harmony gives it a chance to be a masterpiece.

Ask yourself how others—from those in your family to the cashier who serves you at the grocery store—would describe you. If they were to put their relationship with you in the context of color on a painting, what would they say? Would they describe a gray, gloomy day or would they speak of you like the yellow of the sun? "The way of the righteous is like the first gleam of dawn, which shines ever brighter until the full light of day." (Proverbs 4:18) No doubt you're also thinking of how you see others in your life, and you should. You may have quickly realized you have allowed some relationships to develop that may have a negative effect on your life as a masterpiece. Thankfully, there is someone you can turn to for perfect guidance on relationships.

Treating people the way Jesus did

Since the relationships on your Life Palette are the color God uses to paint your life canvas, it makes sense that He is the one to give you direction in how to develop healthy relationships though the living example of His Son.

Now, you may be thinking Jesus was pretty harsh on some folks when He said things like "Snakes! Sons of vipers! How will you escape the judgment of hell?" (Matthew 23:33) Christ *did* say those words, but it's important to know the context when He spoke to others in that way. The only times Jesus communicated in such a way was when He was speaking with the religious leaders who were leading people astray. He never spoke abrasively with those He knew and loved, or with those who were seeking to build a relationship with Him. Instead, Jesus always saw the potential in others and developed relationships with them based on that perception. He changed Simon's name to Peter (the "rock") because Christ saw Peter had the potential to be someone of stability, a firm foundation. Ultimately he was. He went from denying Jesus on the night He was betrayed to giving the inaugural message of the New Testament church. Jesus saw the colors of life in Peter when others may have seen grays.

Relationships give life depth and dimension, energy and vibrancy, emotional strength and stability.

If harshness characterizes how you deal with your spouse, kids, boss, employees, or neighbors, know they probably see you as a dark gray on the canvas of their lives. More than likely, they dread seeing or talking with you and your relationship with them is deteriorating, perhaps without you even realizing it. Most people tend to treat a stranger better than those they love the most. I've seen it (and I'm sure I've done it) when seeing a dad, frustrated with his kids, speaking harshly to them in a way he would never get away with, say, a coworker—and then his phone rings and the tone of his voice miraculously changes as he answers with a pleasant "Hello." That example shows you can control your emotions and develop relational skills so God can paint your masterpiece with vibrant colors of life.

In addition to seeing potential, Jesus also communicated as a servant. He said, "For even the Son of Man came not to be served but to serve others and to give his life as a ransom for many." (Mark 10:45) You may protest, "But I don't want to serve. I want to lead!" Yet there has never been a greater leader in this world than Jesus, and He said this about leadership: "The greatest among you must be a servant." (Matthew 23:11)

My friend Virgil is a motivational speaker. He tells the story of a time when a corporation hired him to speak with their sales department.

He spoke about how important it is to be a servant to nurture successful relationships as a salesperson—and that the better servant you are, the better your sales would be. He also said being a servant began at home, and illustrated his point by describing how he would wake up each morning before his wife to make a pot of coffee. He didn't even drink coffee; he was making the coffee just to serve her. Then he would take her a cup while she was still in bed. As Virgil spoke, one of the salespeople responded with disgust. "This is ridiculous," the man said. "I didn't come to hear about this kind of garbage. I want to learn how to have more sales." Without missing a beat, Virgil responded, "I'm glad you said so, sir. You are going to help me prove my point." He then asked if that man's sales manager was in the room. Another gentleman raised his hand. Virgil said to the manager, "I'm willing to bet my pay that he is your worst salesman in this room." The sales manager reluctantly acknowledged Virgil was right.

How could he know? Simple. "The greatest among you must be a servant," and since that's true, it follows that "the worst among you would not be a servant." Make a conscious choice for your Life Palette to follow the example of Jesus. Be a servant in how you act and communicate.

Start close to home

A color wheel is a must-have tool for an artist. On it, there is what's dubbed the "triad" of colors. The most important triad is the primary colors: red, yellow, and blue. Every other color can be mixed from the primaries. In focusing on relationships on your Life Palette, think in terms of a relational color wheel. What are the primary relationships in your life? Family? Close friends? God? In looking at how you speak and how you serve, this is where you want to begin—with the relationships foremost in your life.

As an artist moves away from painting with the primary colors, it's important to continue to use the triad on the color wheel to keep color harmony. The next triad on the wheel is called the secondary color scheme. These are the colors mixed from the primaries: green, orange, and violet. What are the secondary relationships in your life?

Neighbors? Coworkers? Extended family? Then consider the third level on the color wheel, the triad known as the intermediate colors. They consist of yellow green, red orange, blue violet, blue green, yellow orange, and red violet. What relationships are your intermediate ones? The person you see where you get your coffee in the morning? The stylist who cuts your hair? On your Life Palette, think in terms of these three triads: primary, secondary, and intermediate. When you begin with primary relationships and are successful there, you'll automatically start to act and speak better with your secondary and intermediate relationships. The canvas of your life will begin to be full of the colors of life…and others will be attracted to you.

It's all about them

My first day of kindergarten set the tone for my entire school career. At the end of recess—the one thing I excelled at throughout my elementary years—I talked a neighbor friend into giving me a push in a red wagon. As I steered the wagon for the open door of the classroom, the teacher and principal were standing outside the door having a conversation. I simply gave a quick wave and flew on by. Growing up in a small rural community where everyone knew everyone, my mom was quickly informed. She wasn't happy.

You have your own stories of fun and mischief, be it in kindergarten, high school, or college. But with all the required studies and electives, the one class never offered is People Skills 101, a necessary element on your Life Palette. Having great people skills begins with understanding that the primary interest of everyone is, well, themselves. Talking to someone about the thing they are interested in the most will take your people skills to a new level. A few years ago my wife Kathy and I were at a gathering of extended family, most of whom we really didn't know all that well. Throughout the evening, we simply asked everyone we met a few questions about their lives and each shared very willingly. After the event, we talked about how much we'd learned about everyone, from their jobs and families to their best and worst life experiences. Then Kathy asked me something that made us realize the importance of developing people skills. "Did anyone ask you anything about your life?" I thought for a moment and realized that not one person had asked a single question about me. She said the same was true of her. We knew a lot about them, but they knew nothing about us.

While we are introverts and perfectly fine not talking about ourselves, we were amazed that how, with a few simple questions, people who didn't know us (or even try to get to know us) were willing to share so much about their lives. Why? We asked them about their primary interest in life: themselves. As you learn to do this, people will be drawn to you, and you will be able to develop relationships on your Life Palette that God will use to paint your masterpiece.

Between the Palette Scrapings with Phil Starke

You can create color harmony by using a little of all three primaries in every color you mix, but one has to dominate; then it will harmonize with the other. One relationship I mix in with every relationship is God: He is the dominate relationship in my life that brings harmony to all my relationships.

Encourage, don't discourage

The second step to having great people skills is to always encourage and not discourage. Some people act like God has given them the gift of criticism. That gift is not in the Bible. Criticism only leads to discouragement, while in the Bible Paul said, "So encourage each other and build each other up." (1 Thessalonians 5:11) Notice Paul didn't say, "Here's a good idea. Try to encourage one another every once in a while." He was emphatic in his statement. This is the way you are to live. The more you encourage others, the more they will encourage you in return.

If you're a self-proclaimed critic, you probably have very few friends because no one likes to be around critical people. "But that's just who I am," you may say. *Change*. It's keeping you from your destiny. Be disciplined in this area. God has given you the Spirit of self-control (Galatians 5:23). If you are a natural encourager, be sure to be authentic. "If your gift is to encourage others, be encouraging." (Romans 12:8) If your encouragement is not sincere, it will feel like a bait and switch. For the sake of wanting to be encouraging, I have found many people lie, thinking they are trying to encourage. I served as a worship leader before becoming a pastor. A few times each year we would have tryouts for band members and singers to be on the music team. To see how people would respond to being on stage and in front of people, I would have them audition in front of one another. During one such tryout there was a lady who sang. She was off pitch the entire time and her style did not match the music our church played. While she was sincere in her efforts to worship God with music, it was not the right fit. Yet I was surprised as we closed the session to hear many of the other members telling her how great she did and encouraging her to be on the team. I thought maybe I was the one who had the bad hearing and privately asked them about it. They told me they were just being nice and that I'd better make sure she didn't make the team. In an effort to encourage her, they actually lied…and made me the bad guy. When I told her she didn't make the team, she began quoting all the other folks who tried out and praised her singing ability. It was an awkward moment that proved the value of being authentic in our encouragement.

> **Having great people skills begins with understanding that the primary interest of everyone is themselves.**

One way to encourage is to simply express appreciation. Appreciation is like mixing a vibrant color for a painting. It will add life. Some find it hard to appreciate those who are not just like them. But imagine a painting made of only one color; say, all reds. While it may be a great exercise for an artist to paint with only one color to develop skills in painting values, most of us would not be drawn to such a painting, nor would we want to hang it on the walls of our homes or offices. Discover and appreciate how God has created each of us so uniquely different, and then express appreciation for that. God celebrates it and so should we.

As you make genuine encouragement a part of your daily life, incredible benefits will also be added to your Life Palette. In the Bible, 2 Corinthians 13:11 says, "Be joyful. Grow to maturity. Encourage each other. Live in harmony and peace. Then the God of love and peace will be with you." All of us need encouraging people in our lives. The world beats us down enough to also have people in our primary, secondary, and intermediate relationships do the same. We need to be built up… and we need to build up others.

WHAT ARE YOU SOWING?

I grew up on my grandparent's farm. I learned so much from watching my grandfather tend the land; everything he did in the natural realm of living has taught me so much about the relational and spiritual realms. Every year he would plant two crops: corn and soy beans. Every year when it was time to harvest, he would reap corn and soy beans. Never once in all the years watching and helping him farm did I hear my grandfather say something like, "I planted corn, but looks like the good Lord is giving us sweet peas instead for our harvest." It's an undeniable truth: if you plant corn, you can rest assured you will reap a harvest of corn; if you plant soy beans, you will reap a harvest of soy beans.

The relationships on your Life Palette will yield for you a harvest based on what you sow into them. It is a biblical principle that will add value to every area of your Life Palette once it's understood and put into practice. "You will always harvest what you plant." (Galatians 6:7) Make the next seven relational principles, seen in Jesus' life and throughout Scripture, a part of your *every* interaction with others. You'll ensure all your relationships are always adding value to your Life Palette (and that you're adding value to the Life Palette of others).

1. Always show respect to others. While it may not be the cultural norm, the Bible teaches us to "respect everyone." (1 Peter 2:17) You may think, "Peter didn't know the people I have to deal with." Remember, you will reap what you plant—and the harvest of your life is revealed on your life's canvas. Disrespect will show up as a color that doesn't belong. It will take away from the color harmony God is painting into the masterpiece that is you.

2. Always respond to those who are rude by being polite. It's natural to want to retaliate against those who are offensive to you. However, that'll never add value to your Life Palette. It will only cause disharmony and make things worse in the relationship. When you're rude, it's as though you've thrown a big blob of black into the middle of the canvas that has no business being there. Romans 12:17 says, "Never pay back evil with more evil. Do things in such a way that everyone can see you are honorable."

3. Always be grateful, not demanding. You've chosen to take on the character trait of Jesus and serve others, yet there will always be times when you are being served as well. How you respond to others when they serve you reveals your character. "Do to others as you would like them to do to you." (Luke 6:31) As a pastor, I like to take prospective leaders for the church to a restaurant and see how they treat the person serving them. Anyone can be rude and demanding, but only those who are living life as a masterpiece will consistently choose to be grateful and understanding.

4. Always speak the truth in love. Ephesians 4:15 says that as you speak the truth in love you will be "growing in every way more and more like Christ." Someone may pride themselves on always speaking the truth (or persistently speaking their mind). However, the key to this relational principle is the "in love" part. If you needed surgery to remove cancer from your body, a sharp, smooth scalpel would be preferred to a serrated kitchen knife. Both would have the same result, but one would leave a smaller scar and cause less damage. The same is true of how you speak the truth.

5. Always show grace with those whom you disagree. Don't be judgmental just because you don't see eye to eye with someone. In Romans 14:12-13, Paul gives insight into this principle: "Yes, each of us will give a personal account to God. So let's stop condemning each other. Decide instead to live in such a way that you will not cause another believer to stumble and fall." The focus of this principle is how you respond to those in your life that make choices you believe are wrong. You should always speak in such a way to help them grow, develop, and change, but never beat them over the head. Jesus said, "Do not judge others, and you will not be judged. For you will be treated as you treat others. The standard you use in judging is the standard by which you will be judged." (Matthew 7:1-2)

> **As you make genuine encouragement a part of your daily life, incredible benefits will also be added to your Life Palette.**

6. Always choose to forgive. When you feel you've been wronged or hurt, forgive. As you choose to forgive others, it will allow you to live your life in freedom. Follow Jesus' example. Hear His words from the cross about those who were crucifying Him: "Father, forgive them, for they don't know what they are doing." (Luke 23:34) The color of unforgiveness will destroy a masterpiece. You will never be asked to forgive anyone more than you have already been forgiven by Jesus.

7. Always seek to add value. The value of your relationships on your Life Palette will soar as you choose to add value to everyone in your life. You will be a person that others seek out for a relationship. Jesus said He came to give you a rich and satisfying life. How would your relationships change if you set out to be more like Christ to others?

Be generous with these principles in your relationships. Jesus said in Luke 6:38, "The amount you give will determine the amount you get back."

Life Palette

Letter from Christ

I'll always remember the day my first cousin Barb (she'll always be Barbie to me) unexpectedly passed away. We were close in age; she was just three weeks older than I am. Our families did a lot together when we were growing up, and both moved from Ohio to Colorado around the same time. We kept in touch throughout our high school years and did the occasional family gathering. It was important for me to make the trip to Colorado Springs for her funeral.

As a pastor, I have attended and officiated many funerals, but I've never been to one like Barbie's. There were nearly 1,000 people in attendance, many of whom were under the age of 30. She was a high school math teacher. She made such a positive impact on every student that entered her classroom, they not only attended the funeral, but hundreds wrote letters of appreciation and thanks, all with a similar theme. "I looked forward to going to your classroom." "You were always there to cheer me up." "You made a big difference in my life."

Her coworkers spoke as positively of Barbie as did her own children. In fact, to have met Barbie was to have loved her. She was passionate about people and her relationships with them. She genuinely cared for others. Her life was lived as a masterpiece. It was clear during the few days we were with family and friends at the funeral that the colors on the canvas of her life were the people she impacted.

How does one person make such an incredible impact on everyone she meets? Barbie's greatest passion was that she was a Jesus follower. Everyone who spoke of her life or wrote a letter thanked her for taking the time to pray for them and to share the love of Jesus with them. She was, as Paul says in 2 Corinthians 3:3, "a letter from Christ." The more you live your life as a letter from Christ, the more you will add color to your Life Palette for God to paint your life as a masterpiece.

Jesus led the way in color harmony for our Life Palette by not only showing us how to have relationships with others, but also by pursing a relationship with each of us. In addition, He also set the standard for each of us in an area many of us think is beyond our capability—creativity—but is actually a part of everyone's DNA. Before you talk yourself out of it, read on and discover how creativity is in your nature.

Palette Points

Healthy relationships on your Life Palette bring harmony into your life. How are your relationships affecting your life as a masterpiece? Prayerfully consider the relationships on your Life Palette that you need to focus on building—and perhaps those you need to eliminate.

1. After seeing how Jesus treated people—how he spoke to them and served them—rate your relational harmony ("1" is "not at all like Jesus," while "10" is "a lot like Jesus."

    a) Primary relationships: family, close friends, God?
    b) Secondary relationships: neighbors, coworkers, extended family?
    c) Intermediate relationships: the person who serves you at the coffee shop, or your hair stylist?

    Remember, the better you are with your primary relationships, the better you will be with others.

2. You are a "letter for Christ" to the world. Write a letter that you would hope someone would write about you at your memorial service. Begin to live toward that each day.

3. Look back at the seven relational principles in this chapter. Which one of these do you need to begin implementing the most?

    - Always show respect to others.
    - Always respond to those who are rude by being polite.
    - Always be grateful, not demanding.
    - Always speak the truth in love.
    - Always show grace with those whom you disagree.
    - Always choose to forgive.
    - Always seek to add value.

My One Priority regarding relationships on my Life Palette:

Action Plan:

Chapter Seven

Creativity

I never outgrew fast food, and it's possible I've taken my obsession a bit too far. You see, I've actually learned the ordering systems of fast food restaurants. You could accurately say I'm a pro at knowing what I can and can't order at the different franchises. So when I went through the drive-thru of one of my favorite places one afternoon and ordered my burger just the way I wanted it, I had the opportunity to stretch a young lady's view of life and living.

I placed the order, carefully adding and subtracting everything I wanted on the sandwich to ensure the burger was perfect for my sophisticated food palate. Suddenly, there was a long pause. I thought perhaps the speaker was dead, but a moment later the young lady came back on the speaker and told me I couldn't special order my burger.

Imagine my shock. I knew my system (and my commercials) and believed beyond a shadow of a doubt the restaurant could not only place the order, but deliver the burger exactly to my specifications. After all, I'd done so many times before, and at that location. In a very polite way (for many kids, fast food is their first job so I give them a *lot* of grace), I asked her why I couldn't get my burger prepared the way I wanted. Her response was a first—and though I'd never heard it before, I think it's indicative of how most people limit their lives.

She said, "I don't have a button on my computer for that."

I refrained from laughing out loud. I also realized I was being handed a teaching moment that, if the young lady would be patient with me, would reveal the future was much bigger and offered more opportunities than she could ever imagine. In my most encouraging voice, I told her she didn't need a button for my order, and I had absolute confidence she could ring up my meal and make sure the other staff made my burger just the way I'd asked. I assured her this was not new territory, and if the hundreds of people who'd taken my order before could do it without a specific button, she could, too. Guess what? She did…and the burger was delicious.

The sad truth is, the young lady's view of what she could or couldn't accomplish is the way most people view life. They've trained themselves to look for the button someone else has programmed for them, thinking it's the only way to achieve their goals. They've bought into the lie they're not creative enough to do what they desire, so when the button isn't found, they assume there's simply no way for them to do it. They feel their dream is impossible, even if it's something God is leading them to do.

Between the Palette Scrapings with Phil Starke

As an artist, creativity comes from experiences. You can't simply depend on the tools you learned in art school. The more you paint, the more creative you will be—so paint.

That's simply not true. Jesus Himself said, "I tell you the truth, if you have faith as small as a mustard seed, you can say to this mountain, 'Move from here to there' and it will move. Nothing will be impossible for you." (Matthew 17:20 NIV) Scripture also says, "It is impossible to please God without faith." (Hebrews 11:6) In order to live a life where nothing is impossible for you, start by putting your faith in God through Jesus, then trust in Him that all things are possible by realizing *who you are* in Him. "Anyone who belongs to Christ has become a new person. The old life is gone; a new life has begun!" (2 Corinthians 5:17) Other Bible translations call this becoming "a new creation." And we are this new creation, created in God's image: "Then God said, 'Let us make human beings in our image, to be like us.'" (Genesis 1:26); that is to say, created to take on His character as His sons and daughters—to be His masterpiece.

Do you see the fantastic progression there? One of the characteristics of God innate in each of us as His crea*tion* is we are crea*tive*. God is the Creator and, therefore, defines creativity. To not believe this is to close your eyes to all He has created. In my painting "Rock Climbers," you can see one of the beautiful Saguaro cactuses that grow near my home. They grow in the countryside around us like pine trees grow in a forest. It's genius! As a landscape artist, I will never run out of fresh, creative ideas by simply looking at all God has done in nature. Consider the variety of wildlife on earth, how infinitely genius God's creativity must have been to make a giraffe with its long neck, an elephant with its enormous poise, or a powerful lion as the "king of the jungle." Or imagine the vastness of space and what little we know about the universe. If humans could learn to travel at the speed of light or zoom in and out of wormholes like in sci-fi movies, we still couldn't begin to fully explore all God has created because creativity is a part of His very core.

You may not be artistic; that's another matter altogether, but you are creative. It's part of your DNA.

Creativity is one of the key elements necessary on your Life Palette in order to be the masterpiece God destined you to be. You only need to tap into the creativity that's already placed within you, at your core, by your Creator. It's heartbreaking to hear people speak of themselves as not being creative, but it's something I hear all the time. One of the primary reasons people don't see themselves as creative is that they narrowly define a creative person as someone who is an artist or a musician—but creativity is as vast as God Himself. Because you are created in His image, you, too, inherit His ability to be creative! You don't need a button. You have the capability to actually *make* one!

No one has received the fullness of God's creativity; we are not, after all, the Creator. But we do possess His characteristic of creativity working within the gifted abilities and personality that He designed within each one of us. While one person may be a creative genius in the arts, others will be a creative genius in business, or parenting, or teaching…the list goes on. To see yourself as anything less than creative in your area of pursuit is to miss out on masterpiece living and reaching the full potential He has for you.

As you develop your Life Palette, choose to make creativity in all your endeavors a priority. It's in you—and will take you further than you ever dreamed. In the Bible, Paul encourages you to "put on your new nature, and be renewed as you learn to know your Creator and become like him." (Colossians 3:10) Begin by asking God in prayer to open your heart and mind to the vastness of the creativity He has placed within you.

It's a God thing

Creativity is completely and fully "a God thing." We see it in the triune nature of God, more commonly called the Trinity:

God the Father began everything on this earth: "In the beginning God created…" (Genesis 1:1) The more we engage in the process of creativity in our lives, the more we are joining with Him in this divine activity: we live in God, and He lives in us. (1 John 4:16)

As God the Father's only Son, Jesus Christ modeled creativity as an example for us. "Jesus always used stories and illustrations like these when speaking to the crowds. In fact, he never spoke to them without using such parables. This fulfilled what God had spoken through the prophet: 'I will speak to you in parables. I will explain things hidden since the creation of the world.'" (Matthew 13:34-35) Christ never spoke or performed ministry without incorporating creativity.

It's sad to consider how many folks feel called into Christian ministry work, yet never utilize creativity as they minister. Can you imagine anyone ever sleeping through one of Jesus' sermons? This is not just for pastors or evangelists. Whatever you are doing with your life is your ministry if you're a follower of Christ. You may be a night shift janitor at a warehouse; a truck driver or a software engineer; an airline pilot or a treasure hunter; a farmer or in government work—whatever it is you're gifted at doing or choosing to do, that *is* your ministry. "And whatever you do or say, do it as a representative of the Lord Jesus, giving thanks through him to God the Father." (Colossians 3:17) "Work willingly at whatever you do, as though you were working for the Lord rather than for people." (Colossians 3:23) To live your life without being open to God's creativity in your chosen field—your ministry—is to choose to live as less than the masterpiece He has created you to be.

The Holy Spirit empowers us with creativity. "For the Lord is the Spirit, and wherever the Spirit of the Lord is, there is freedom. So all of us who have had that veil removed can see and reflect the glory of the Lord. And the Lord—who is the Spirit—makes us more and more like him as we are changed into his glorious image." (2 Corinthians 3:17-18) Since part of the nature and character of God is creativity, and we are created in His image and through His Spirit made to reflect Him in all we do and say, the question is not, "How do I become creative?" Rather it's this: "What is hindering me from releasing the creativity God has placed within me?" Creativity is woven into the fabric of your being.

What's keeping creativity from being a major part of your Life Palette? Perhaps you're like the young lady waiting on me in the drive-thru, looking for a button to push. No one has ever helped you realize the creative potential that's lurking deep within your heart and abilities. Or maybe it was driven out of your life, banished starting from a very early age. Much of life for children is about conforming to the norm, whatever that may be. Yet masterpieces are never conforming or normal.

Outside the lines

When each of my kids began coloring, I encouraged them to be expressive and free in the use of their crayons. I knew it would affect their Life Palette positively if they saw themselves as being creative. I can't tell you how many times I've had a teacher, children's pastor, or a well-meaning person talk with me critically about my kids' inability to color within the lines. I kindly and patiently explain to them how and why I never taught my kids to color within the lines, and then say how I'd appreciate it if they wouldn't limit them in that way.

The more you were told to stay within the lines, the more you began to shift from being creative to confined, from artistic to analytical, from laughter to logic, from imagination to routine. It's not that there is anything wrong with boundaries: God created many boundaries for good, but you can't allow them to trap you in areas of your life where He designed you to live without limits. It's not that being analytical is bad. You may need to be better at analyzing situations. But without creativity, you often cannot see beyond the problem you're trying to figure out. It's not that logic is inappropriate; quite the contrary. But when logic kills the creative seed within, it will also put to death the imagination that inspires you to try to do the thing that seems impossible; that thing is fueled by faith. Routine is not wrong, but to allow it to steal the creative potential on your Life Palette is to live in a rut that will lead to a dull and lifeless existence.

When you were taught as a child to color within the lines, it wasn't that anyone was purposefully trying to squelch the creativity God put within you—but it did. It was as though you were being told you needed to have a "button" to get anything done. Inside the parameters of God's holiness, there are no lines. You are a masterpiece waiting to express the very nature of God in your area of choosing—career, relationships, all of life—through creativity. Everyone is telling you to conform to their standard, not wanting you to get ahead of them or be better at something than they are. God, though, wants to free you to express His greatness through your creativity.

Break free!

Ready to bust loose from the prison of conformity and begin to explore the creative genius God has placed within the core of your being? It's time for creativity to be a part of your Life Palette so God can paint your life with colors you've never even dreamed of. Here are six ways you can make that happen:

1. Quit making excuses. Don't tell yourself, "I'm just not creative." Remember, you're made in the image of God; you have His Spirit living within you. The reality is most people reason away their creativity with this excuse because they're frightened and intimidated by even the thought of being creative. You may not be artistic; that's another matter altogether, but you *are* creative. It's part of your DNA.

2. Choose to be optimistic. This does not mean taking a view that everything in life is rosy or will "somehow work out" regardless of the circumstances. Optimistic creativity means you look for the best solutions even when you're in the worst circumstances. Maybe you need to discover what the Lord wants you to learn as you go through something tough.

It would be untrue to say the only time you're creative is when you are optimistic. You can also be creatively negative or evil. The key for your Life Palette is to utilize creative optimism to get the positive results God desires for you. This is closely tied to faith, in that it's highly improbable you'll grow in your faith if you view life through cynical lenses. The apostle Paul said it this way: "No, dear brothers and sisters, I have not achieved it, but I focus on this one thing: Forgetting the past and looking forward to what lies ahead, I press on to reach the end of the race and receive the heavenly prize for which God, through Christ Jesus, is calling us." (Philippians 3:13-14) Notice his optimistic attitude toward the future and eternity. Not recounting the failures of the past or allowing them to dictate his present, Paul looked forward to the potential he had through Christ. Think of the story of the fisherman who said if he were going fishing for Moby Dick, he would be sure to take tartar sauce with him on the boat. He was totally expecting to have a meal.

Nothing will kill creativity faster than negativity or pessimism from yourself or others. Choose to be optimistic and creatively look for solutions and possibilities. I love Psalm 77:19 that talks about God leading Moses and the children of Israel through the Red Sea: "Your road led through the sea, your pathway through the mighty waters—a pathway no one knew was there!" Choose optimism to release the creativity God has placed *within* you, and you will discover the pathway God has placed *for* you.

3. Discipline your creative energy. Creativity requires patience. God is disciplined and part of His characteristics for you is *self-discipline*. A masterpiece is not created in haste. It's birthed from the creative, thoughtful patience of a skilled artist. A great symphony is written through the diligence and discipline of a composer. I'm often asked by other artists how I can paint so many paintings so quickly (I paint about 12-15 paintings each month). My answer is simple: I paint. What I mean is I don't wait to feel inspired; if I waited for inspiration, I would rarely paint. I've learned from the coaching of masters that the more I choose to paint from an attitude of discipline, the more creative I am and the more inspired I become. Creativity is nurtured through discipline.

> **Creativity is nurtured through discipline.**

Here's something I do away from the canvas. When facing a problem, I'll prayerfully discipline myself to write out up to 25 solutions before I consider making a decision: the greater the problem, the higher my total of potential solutions. Often, many of my ideas are ridiculous, unaffordable, and improbable; however, that sort of creative discipline always paves the way to creative solutions that work. I'll also brainstorm with people who have tapped into their God-given creativity. My wife Kathy is one of the most creative thinkers I know. In any brainstorm session, she will come up with creative ideas I never considered. My staff is always looking for creative solutions to any problem. I love to sit with them and brainstorm ideas and possibilities. The key to having successful brainstorming sessions is to realize there are no stupid ideas. It's alright to put whatever comes to mind on the table, regardless how "out of this world" it may be. Often someone throws out a crazy idea that stimulates a new idea in another person in the room. Together, we are then able to develop the ideas to a creative practical solution and put with it a strategy that's doable. The more time you spend brainstorming, the more productive you'll be.

Be sure to also take time to pray, read the Bible, and ask God to show you creative solutions through His Word. Lastly, try to choose those in your inner circle carefully. You've probably been with a group of people where someone came up with a great idea, only to have it shot down by a person who was negative or always looking at the downside. Part of the discipline of being creative is guarding who you allow to influence your life.

4. Have intentionality. I once had the privilege of traveling with several friends from our church up to Northern Canada to go fishing. My first trip north of the border was also the first time I ever fished with a guide. I was amazed by how they intentionally set our bait to catch a certain fish. When they said it was time to fish for Walleye, they changed the bait and how we fished—and we caught Walleye. When the Walleye wasn't biting, it was time for a bait change so we could catch Pike. No sooner had we started trolling, the tug would come on the line and we caught Pike. We weren't just putting a worm on the hook and hoping a fish was hungry. Our guides knew how to bait and set the hooks so we caught what we wanted. It was very intentional.

Creativity requires being intentional. While you may have the accidental creative moment, that's not the norm. Most people who appear to be creative geniuses intentionally set aside time to do the discipline of being creative and never make a decision without intentionally focusing on creativity. Force yourself to see all things through creative eyes. Much like an artist sees everything and asks themselves how they might paint it, or what colors they would mix to get the color they are seeing, strive to look at your life the same way. Ask God to unleash this in your daily life and help you see new ways of doing things—new angles, a new path or roadway through a problem, or a new way to improve what is already successful. Paul said it this way: "I run with purpose in every step. I am not just shadowboxing." (1 Corinthians 9:26)

5. Depart from the norm. I went to lunch one day with a friend. We made plans to meet at his office and then go to a nearby sandwich shop that he loved, but I had never been to before. When we got to the shop I asked him what was good, planning to lean on his recommendation. He responded by telling me that the first time he visited the restaurant several years earlier, he ordered a particular sandwich and enjoyed it so much, it's the only sandwich he's ever ordered since then. I was surprised and immediately offered to buy his lunch on one condition: he had to try anything from the menu except the one sandwich he always ordered. Guess what? He wanted the same sandwich so badly he paid for his own lunch.

It's so easy to get into a rut and never have variety in life. Yet if we never depart from the norm to try new things, not only will we not experience new and creative ideas, but we will actually begin to shut down the creative genius God has placed within us.

Look at how Jesus healed the blind on two different occasions, first in Mark 10:51-52. "'What do you want me to do for you?' Jesus asked. 'My rabbi,' the blind man said, 'I want to see!' And Jesus said to him, 'Go, for your faith has healed you.' Instantly the man could see, and he followed Jesus down the road." Then consider the account from John 9:6-7. "Then he spit on the ground, made mud with the saliva, and spread the mud over the blind man's eyes. He told him, 'Go wash yourself in the pool of Siloam' (Siloam means "sent"). So the man went and washed and came back seeing!" Christ used creativity to heal the blind. Had He always used the same words, "Go, your faith has healed you," people might have thought all they had to do was use those magic words and, abracadabra, healing would happen! Had Jesus only used the mud method, well...wouldn't it be interesting to see that tried in church today? The point is there is no *one* way to do something great. Christ continued to minister with creativity throughout His life on earth and, arguably, is just as creative today as He influences people's lives from heaven.

As you choose to depart from the norm, it will open up creative thinking in your life. Some of the ways I do this is to take a different route home whenever I can, even if it's longer. I'll pray at different times to avoid getting in a spiritual rut. I'll try different restaurants and order something new (I can't eat fast food *all* the time). Creativity requires faith to overcome the fear of the unknown, which leads to the final thing necessary to break free from the bonds of normality.

6. Take more risk. The enemy of creativity is fear of failure, always playing it safe because we know we can do something but we're not sure if we can—or want—to go to the next level. Masterpiece living is all about reaching new heights, which means getting creative and taking risk. And here's something that'll help you do it! When you're creative, you will sometimes fail. *Embrace* it. You'll have some really stupid ideas. *Love* it. Because from those failures and stupid ideas will come the genius of success and the ideas that work and will take you higher.

My daughter Kadi is also an artist, and she's fearless when it comes to painting with color. She was in an art show at our local college when she was in high school, and her pieces stood out compared to the other students because of her use of color. Kadi's art teacher told me that she never had a student who was so bold when it came to color.

> **The more you are willing to risk and take creative chances, the more you will attract others to your life and vision.**

Most artists play it safe and are afraid to put bold colors on the canvas, believing they will ruin the painting. Most people, like those timid artists, find a system that works for their life and become afraid to creatively consider a change or improvement because of the potential of ruining what they already have. Yet that fear will keep them from being like Kadi and experiencing the joy and freedom of new and bold colors in their lives. Her paintings attracted everyone who attended the show. The more you are willing to risk and take creative chances, the more you will attract others to your life and vision. People follow and look toward those who are fearless and are willing to try something new.

Look at these verses from The Message Bible regarding what Jesus had to say about faith and risk:

Life Palette

"Jesus turned—caught her at it. Then he reassured her: 'Courage, daughter. You took a risk of faith, and now you're well.' The woman was well from then on." (Matthew 9:21-22)

"That stumped them, literalists that they were. Unwilling to risk losing face again in one of these public verbal exchanges, they quit asking questions for good." (Matthew 22:46)

"Our lives are at constant risk for Jesus' sake, which makes Jesus' life all the more evident in us." (2 Corinthians 4:11)

Between the Palette Scrapings with Phil Starke

Painting *en plein air* develops creativity for an artist because you have to interpret life. If you only paint from photos, you are in danger of simply becoming a copier. In the same way, God uses your life experiences to make you more creative—if you allow Him.

Creativity is all about doing things differently than usual. In Luke 5, there's a great story of a few guys who risked doing things differently to get their friend to Jesus. "When they could not find a way to do this because of the crowd, they went up on the roof and lowered him on his mat through the tiles into the middle of the crowd, right in front of Jesus. When Jesus saw their faith, he said, 'Friend, your sins are forgiven…I tell you, get up, take your mat and go home.' Immediately he stood up in front of them, took what he had been lying on and went home praising God." (Luke 5:19-20, 24-25 NIV) Their willingness to risk led their friend to freedom and life.

Let God unleash your creativity

Make creativity a lifestyle on your Life Palette. Scripture says, "And now, just as you accepted Christ Jesus as your Lord, you must continue to follow him. Let your roots grow down into him, and let your lives be built on him. Then your faith will grow strong in the truth you were taught, and you will overflow with thankfulness." (Colossians 2:6-7)

Ask God to unleash the creativity He has placed within your life. Decide right this moment to carve out some time to sit and focus on being creative. Discover the environments that inspire your creativity. God created everything that exists, so "set your sights on the realities of heaven, where Christ sits in the place of honor at God's right hand. Think about the things of heaven, not the things of earth." (Colossians 3:1-2) Deal harshly with earthly realities that kill your creativity: "So put to death the sinful, earthly things lurking within you." (Colossians 3:5) Let God release and renew the creativity He has put in the core of your being!

As you make creativity a part of your Life Palette, it will be reflected on the canvas of your life. The more you reflect creativity, the more you reflect the character and nature of God. To reflect the nature and character of God is truly the ultimate achievement in living life as His masterpiece. While creativity is a big part of it all, it's only that—a part. To be creative in a way that would be most characteristic of God, you must also learn to be consistent.

Palette Points

Creativity is a part of your very core and a key element for living as the masterpiece God created you to be. Release the creative genius God has placed in you.

1. Think through the excuses you use to tell yourself you are not creative. What can you begin to do to reprogram your thinking regarding these excuses? For each excuse, formulate a plan of action to overcome it. Remember, be optimistic!

2. Begin disciplining your creative energy. Take one area of your life, work, relationships, finances—pick any area—where you feel you're in a rut. Write down at least 25 ideas for getting out of that rut. Start big, and write it down even if it's unrealistic, too expensive, or never been done before. Then you will begin to come up with some ideas you can implement in your action plan. If you cannot do this on your own, get a group of friends who will walk you through the process.

3. What one risk have you been avoiding that you believe could catapult you forward in your life? What do you need to do to step out and take that risk today?

My One Priority regarding creativity on my Life Palette:

Action Plan:

Chapter Eight

Consistency

The good news is God leads the way for us in consistency: "Jesus Christ is the same yesterday, today, and forever." (Hebrews 13:8) While we may not think often about this character quality in God, we're grateful He is a never-changing God, perfect in all His ways.

One of the things that attracted me to paint the painting "Down Country Roads" is the contrast of the mountain standing tall and strong in the background—and the thought of knowing when you wake up in the morning it will still be standing against the temporal buildings in the foreground. It's never-changing and consistent, like God.

But what would it be like if God were *not* consistent? Imagine waking up this morning and wondering whether or not God decided to become evil overnight and if He would ever be trustworthy again? If He were anything but consistent, we would be painfully aware of the days of inconsistency—and we would dread them. In the midst of difficulties, when we need His presence and power the most, we'd have to deal with the possibility that God might be having an "off" day; that even though Jesus said in Matthew 28:20, "I am with you always, even to the end of the age," He may not actually be there at that particular moment.

While we will never be perfect in all our ways here on this earth, there are some things that we can do daily to improve our consistency, allowing our lives to better reflect the nature and character of God as His masterpiece. Consider the word "daily" as an acrostic: **D**ream daily, **A**dvance daily, **I**nitiate daily, **L**earn daily and **Y**ield daily. The key to consistency being a part of your Life Palette is to do things daily.

As an artist, I spend a lot of time with other artists who are very committed to the process of creativity, but often at the expense of doing what is needed daily to paint a masterpiece. The most creative people I know are also the most consistent people I know. They are disciplined and dependable. Their daily habits are the very things that open the doors to their greatest creative genius. The artists who paint masterpieces are the artists who consistently paint. Those who consider themselves creative geniuses—waiting for a moment of inspiration to pick up their brushes and put paint on the canvas—rarely paint. And when they do, they often find their skill to apply the paint woefully lacking.

Between the Palette Scrapings with Phil Starke

If you are going to wait around for inspiration before you paint, you'll hardly ever paint. I choose to get up and paint every day. I commit to goals and discipline. God uses that to lead to creativity in and through my painting.

I'm the type of person who evaluates and sets goals at the beginning of each year. Actually, I tend to do most of my goal setting in early December so I can have a plan finalized and in place by the start of January. I tend to see New Year's Day as the first day toward living out my new goals; it's a launching point, not just a day for hanging out with friends and family. I work at setting goals in several different areas I know are important for my Life Palette: spiritual, relational (including those with my wife, children, and friendships), physical, and for my aspirations in my ministry and my art.

One time, while I was prayerfully considering my goals as an artist for the coming year, I took time to read through what some other artists I knew were trying to accomplish in their lives. For the most part, it was inspiring and challenging, but I came across one artist whose goal for the year spoke very clearly as to *why* she was where she was. She said she was planning on working on the three paintings started the previous year and was hoping to finish them. She also stated this goal was "aggressive." Her goal told me she was either the slowest painter alive, or she did not paint consistently. I like to finish three paintings a *week*. The discipline of "daily" is the key to consistency, and without consistency on your Life Palette, masterpiece living will be a wish rather than a reality.

Five D.A.I.L.Y. habits for success

The "D" in our D.A.I.L.Y. acrostic stands for **Dream**. In chapter four, we looked at Joseph and his dreams and their place of importance in determining our values. Here we want to solidify them for our daily success. For some, this will be a discipline; for others, it'll be a great joy, done with ease. To dream daily means to *focus on and expand* the dream God has given you as His masterpiece. The sad reality is that by the time most people reach their mid-thirties, they've had such a tremendous dose of reality they've given up on the dreams that once burned in their hearts.

The dreams God places in you are a precious commodity that must be protected and cultivated. For many, the dream must be rediscovered and rekindled. If you feel you've lost your dreams—or that you have no dreams at all—stop reading a moment and allow yourself time to dream. Think back to when you were younger, maybe even as far back as your childhood, and consider what you dreamed about back then.

We're not talking here of a passing fancy, such as what you wanted to be when you grew up. As a child I was a big Cleveland Browns football fan and, like many boys growing up in the Buckeye state in the late 1960s, I played football in school. If you asked me what I wanted to be in the moments after the Browns won (especially when they beat their rival, the Cincinnati Bengals), I would say I wanted to be a pro football player. With each sports season, the profession would change. Baseball, then back to football, with maybe a fireman or even an astronaut thrown in after watching fellow Buckeye Neil Armstrong walk on the moon on my folk's black and white television. Yet as I grew into my early teen years, I realized that while I enjoyed all those things, none were the driving passion I dreamed about every day. I began to realize I had hopes and desires that were consistently a part of my daily dreams regardless of the sports season or the latest movie. Those are the kind of dreams you need to consider.

Maybe you had a sixth grade teacher who made a major impact in your life and you began to dream of teaching sixth graders, but somewhere along the way you were told you would never be good enough to get into college—and the dream slowly died. Or perhaps you always dreamed of starting your own business and providing jobs for others in your community, but when you began to pursue it a friend said you'd never be able to afford your own business. You took a job to start saving, and the other demands of life took over—and the dream slowly died.

God celebrates those dreams in you. You may have moments, fleeting at best, when you remember that special thing you wanted to do in life, but the pain of the death of that dream is so hard you quickly put it out of your mind. Take some time to prayerfully ask God to help you recall and rekindle that dream once more, the one He has for you as His masterpiece. Let that dream come alive again. Others may not understand, but this is about *you* living as the masterpiece God created you to be. Remember, God gave Joseph a dream, a vision for his life, and his brothers taunted him. "Here comes the dreamer!" they said. (Genesis 37:19) Yet as Joseph daily pursued the dream God gave him, it came to pass.

When the dreams of God are clearly re-birthed in your heart and mind, how do you go about protecting and developing them? What do you do when your daily life doesn't appear to be headed toward the dream and masterpiece God has for you? You develop D.A.I.L.Y. habits on your Life Palette. The things you do daily will determine your success or failure at achieving and maintaining His dream for you.

A FULFILLED DREAM TAKES TIME

Of course, dreaming alone isn't enough. It's the things you *do* every day to live the dream that's important. Most people get discouraged and

LIFE PALETTE

Desert Song
30 x 48"
Location: Old Marana, Arizona
Appeared in Western Art Collector Magazine, July 2012

April Morning
9 x 12"
Location: Oro Valley, Catalina Mountains, *en plein air*

To view or purchase Jeff's art, check out www.jeffloveart.com

Life Palette

Drift And Meander
24 x 30"
Location: Old Marana, Arizona

Hidden Beauty
24 x 36"
Location: Bowman Lake, Glacier National Park

LIFE PALETTE

In The Footsteps Of The Giant
24 x 30"
Location: East Rosebud Creek, Montana (Commission)

Into The Morning
11 x 14"
Location: Near the Arizona-Sonora Desert Museum, Saguaro National Park

To view or purchase Jeff's art, check out www.jeffloveart.com

Life Palette

Luminous Splendor
24 x 30"
Location: Grand Teton National Park

Parked In The Barn
24 x 30"
Location: Farm outside of Florence, Oregon

To view or purchase Jeff's art, check out www.jeffloveart.com

give up on their God-given dream because of one simple element that's a vital and undeniable part of seeing any dream come to pass: time. All great dreams take time.

One of my favorite leaders in Scripture is Joshua. The Bible book that bears his name begins with him taking the reins of leadership over the children of Israel. "After the death of Moses the Lord's servant, the Lord spoke to Joshua son of Nun, Moses' assistant. He said, 'Moses my servant is dead. Therefore, the time has come for you to lead these people, the Israelites, across the Jordan River into the land I am giving them.'" (Joshua 1:1-2) That was an incredible moment! Joshua was about to see the fulfillment of a dream that started 40 years earlier when Moses sent him and 11 others into the Promised Land as spies. The set up for this moment—for this dream fulfilled—was that the people of Israel were slaves for 400 years and it weakened them as a people. Moses sent a dozen spies into the Promised Land to scope things out, but only two of them returned enthusiastic about going into the land: Caleb and Joshua. The others couldn't see past the potential problems to the dream God had for them.

> **You are a masterpiece and the dreams He places within you are masterpiece dreams.**

A generation later, only Caleb and Joshua remained from the time God first gave the dream. The other spies, the ones who couldn't see the dream, never saw the Promised Land. How did Joshua hold onto this dream for four decades? How did he stay faithful and protect the dream God gave him as a spy?

The key to successfully dreaming daily is trusting in the promises of God—recognizing that you possess God's promises the same way Joshua did:

Joshua had God's stated purpose. Joshua possessed a commitment from God specifically about the Promised Land. "And I reaffirmed my covenant with them. Under its terms, I promised to give them the land of Canaan, where they were living as foreigners." (Exodus 6:4) I can picture Joshua dreaming of getting back to the Promised Land on a daily basis, his report to Moses after returning from spying out the land echoing in his heart and mind, keeping the dream alive: "We entered the land you sent us to explore, and it is indeed a bountiful country—a land flowing with milk and honey." (Numbers 13:27) Then, when the moment arrives for Joshua to lead the people into the land, God gives him a new commitment: "I promise you what I promised Moses: 'Wherever you set foot, you will be on land I have given you—from the Negev wilderness in the south to the Lebanon mountains in the north, from the Euphrates River in the east to the Mediterranean Sea in the west, including all the land of the Hittites.'" (Joshua 1:3-4)

God's promise for you is found in His stated purpose for you: "For we are God's masterpiece. He has created us anew in Christ Jesus, so we can do the good things he planned for us long ago." (Ephesians 2:10) Remember that daily. Pray that daily. Make it personal and speak it daily. "Heavenly Father, I am your masterpiece. You have created me anew in Christ Jesus. I am doing the good thing you planned for me long ago."

Joshua had the promise of God's presence in his life to encourage him toward the dream daily: "No one will be able to stand against you as long as you live. For I will be with you as I was with Moses." (Joshua 1:5) Some of Jesus' last words to the disciples assure us of the promise of His presence in our lives as well. Remember them from earlier? "And be sure of this: I am with you always, even to the end of the age." (Matthew 28:20) Rely on His presence daily to ensure that the dream He's given you never dies. Tap into His presence through praying daily and reading His Word daily. Ask Him to empower you to clearly see the dream and vision He has for you.

Joshua received the promise of God's faithfulness. "I will not fail you or abandon you." (Joshua 1:5) We see throughout Scripture that God is our faithful Heavenly Father. Paul says it this way in 2 Thessalonians 3:3: "But the Lord is faithful; he will strengthen you and guard you from the evil one." God was faithful to the cause of getting Joshua and the children of Israel into the Promised Land, and He is faithful to the cause of you being and living as His masterpiece. God does not let His promises fail. Yet recall Joshua had one thing required of him: "This is my command—be strong and courageous! Do not be afraid or discouraged. For the Lord your God is with you wherever you go." (Joshua 1:9) The enemy would like nothing more than to discourage you and keep you from dreaming the dream of God daily, to give in to weakness, and give up. Paul encourages you in the same way God did Joshua: "Be strong in the Lord and in his mighty power. Put on all of God's armor so that you will be able to stand firm against all strategies of the devil. For we are not fighting against flesh-and-blood enemies, but against evil rulers and authorities of the unseen world, against mighty powers in this dark world, and against evil spirits in the heavenly places." (Ephesians 6:10-12) Be strong. Stand firm. Dream daily the dream God has for you. As you do, it will lead to living consistently as the masterpiece God created you to be.

That leads us to the A in our D.A.I.L.Y. acrostic toward success, **Advance**. I grew up hearing the well-worn phrase, "Rome wasn't built in a day." As a young person who wanted everything "right now," that was a hard saying to wrap my head around. During my younger years, everything was becoming instant: cooking with the microwave, getting fast food whenever we were hungry, and watching the world move at an ever-increasing pace. Yet a masterpiece takes time to create. Leonardo da Vinci began working on the Mona Lisa in 1503. History tells us he worked on that masterpiece for four years—and even then didn't feel it was finished. The painting sat silent and untouched in his studio for another nine years before he began working on it again, laboring for another three years before his death in 1519. I'm not sure how long it took to build Rome, but I do know that da Vinci didn't paint the Mona Lisa in a day. He was advancing the piece little by little every day he picked up the brush.

The dream God has given you will not be fulfilled in a day. You are a masterpiece and the dreams He places within you are masterpiece dreams. The consistency to advance your dream a little each day is vital on your Life Palette so God can paint the masterpiece He has in mind.

Getting across the Jordan River and into the Promised Land was simply the first step for Joshua and the children of Israel. Once they were in the land, they had to conquer those who were occupying it and robbing them of the dream God had given. Thankfully, He gave Joshua a plan to advance: "Now the gates of Jericho were tightly shut because the people were afraid of the Israelites. No one was allowed to go out or in. But the Lord said to Joshua, 'I have given you Jericho, its king, and all its strong warriors. You and your fighting men should march around the town once a day for six days. Seven priests will walk ahead of the Ark, each carrying a ram's horn. On the seventh day you are to march around the town seven times, with the priests blowing the horns. When you hear the priests give one long blast on the rams' horns, have all the people shout as loud as they can. Then the walls of the town will collapse, and the people can charge straight into the town.'" (Joshua 6:1-5)

> **The best day to take the initiative toward planting your dreams was yesterday. Today is the next best day.**

From a military standpoint, God's plan made no sense. In fact, it was ridiculous. Imagine if the United States was at war and the president announced such a plan to defeat the enemy. He would be mocked and probably impeached. But God was directing Joshua and his army and, much more than military strategy, there was a dream—and the testing of that dream—on the line. There is a masterpiece being created and a need for consistency to advance toward the dream set before them, regardless of the obstacles or what others might say.

The sad truth is many of us live our lives dreaming the dream God has given us without ever advancing one step toward it. Instead, we want to instantly fast forward to the seventh day without having to march the first six days, and we miss the point: the six days of marching is when the masterpiece is in the making, when God is creating in us the character and qualities necessary to live the dream. Don't just hope the dreams of God come true in your life. Prayerfully ask God for His plan and direction to advance daily, to move forward toward the dreams He has for you. Unless you are committed to advancing day by day, you will simply be a daydreamer and impede the progress God wants to see.

Three days before I was born on May 25, 1961, President John F. Kennedy addressed the Congress of the United States. He said, "I believe that this nation should commit itself to achieving the goal, before this decade is out, of landing a man on the moon and returning him safely to the earth." On July 16, 1969, Apollo 11 began the journey from Kennedy Space Center to the moon. Amazingly, four days after liftoff, Neil Armstrong was the first man to set foot on the surface of the moon. America's space program didn't go from President Kennedy's congressional address in 1961 to the moon in 1969 by just dreaming. The dream laid out by the president was advanced every day in between. A dream without the strategy of advancing daily is a dream destined to be unrealized.

The "I" in D.A.I.L.Y. stands for **Initiate**. Consistency on your Life Palette requires you to initiate daily. "Joshua got up early the next morning, and the priests again carried the Ark of the Lord…On the second day they marched around the town once and returned to the camp. They followed this pattern for six days." (Joshua 6:12, 14) I've often wondered what would have happened had Joshua and his army skipped the first days of marching in silence around the city of Jericho. Suppose they decided to simply wait until the seventh day and march around seven times and blow the trumpet?

Something was happening during the first six days of marching. God was at work. He was not only preparing Joshua and the children of Israel, He was using this unusual strategy to create fear and intimidation in the hearts and minds of the enemy as they stood on the walls each day wondering if *this* was the day Joshua would attack. How sad it would be to get to the seventh day, the seventh time around, and not be prepared for what God planned. Imagine if no one had initiated any work toward the dream of reaching the moon and then suddenly it was the last year of the decade. It would have been too late. It is imperative you wake each day with a vigor and enthusiasm of initiating something, even if it's the simplest and seemingly smallest advancement, toward the dream God has for you.

In front of the barn where my grandfather walked daily to feed his sheep are several large trees. I remember when he planted them; the saplings seemed insignificant compared to the big oak and walnut trees next to the barn. Now, after all these years, those saplings are majestic, mature trees. My grandfather's willingness to take the initiative that day provides a picture of a visionary, someone who realized the simplest initiative on one day would be a dream realized in years to come. The best day to take the initiative toward planting your dreams was yesterday. Today is the next best day—so initiate today and every day after this. Live with an expectation that someday a masterpiece will be realized.

The "L" in our D.A.I.L.Y. acrostic stands for **Learn**. To have consistency on your Life Palette, it is imperative that you learn every day. To live as the masterpiece God created you to be, the knowledge you gained yesterday is not enough to advance to tomorrow. Determine to be a lifetime learner.

Between the Palette Scrapings with Phil Starke

We discover our strengths when we start doing things. I volunteer to pull weeds at my church. It's my way of making sure I am serving consistently. I've discovered it to be one of the few quiet moments that allow me to think without distraction, and I find it to be restful.

I'm sometimes shocked when I look at some of the pieces I painted in my early years. I heard the story of one artist who became famous and wealthy. While walking past a gallery in New York City, he noticed one of his early paintings on an easel in the window. He went into the gallery and asked if the painting was for sale. He purchased it, but when asked if he wanted it wrapped, he said it was not necessary—then proceeded to pull out his pocket knife and slice the canvas before their eyes. They were stunned, especially since the artist was highly collected and the purchase price was high. What the gallery owners didn't know was the man who had purchased and destroyed the painting was, in fact, the artist.

Of course, most artists do not have the financial means to go back and purchase the embarrassing pieces from years gone by and destroy them. Instead, the ongoing learning process of an artist is vividly documented on each signed and dated canvas. Far worse, though, than having those "learning pieces" out in the public is to have those pieces reveal that you were not learning at all. For an artist to say he could not tell the difference between his early work and later paintings would be a detrimental statement. In truth, that's an artist you've never heard of, an artist who was not learning daily and improving.

Joshua not only had the dream of occupying the Promised Land, he was willing to learn what was necessary to see the dream come to pass: "Then Joshua secretly sent out two spies from the Israelite camp at Acacia Grove. He instructed them, 'Scout out the land on the other side of the Jordan River, especially around Jericho.'" (Joshua 2:1) This must have been an amazing moment as Joshua, a one-time spy himself, sent out spies to take the very same land. He didn't assume what he'd learned about the land 40 years earlier still applied. He wanted new intelligence. The knowledge of yesterday is of value and worth only if it's married with what you are learning today.

Unless you dedicate yourself to learning daily, you will soon become obsolete and set aside, full of unrealized dreams. I have an uncle and cousins who still farm in Ohio to this day; they are very successful farmers. Their skills and knowledge are directly founded in the farming my grandfather did, yet the way they go about it today is vastly different. While grandpa was successful as a farmer in his day, someone still trying to do things the way he did it would not be competitive today.

Humility is also a necessary ingredient for those who are learners. If you feel you are not humble by nature, then you will likely struggle to learn and grow. Prayerfully ask God for the strength to be a humble and teachable learner.

Lastly, "Y" stands for **Yield** daily to God, your master artist. "Joshua told the people, 'Consecrate yourselves, for tomorrow the Lord will do amazing things among you.'" (Joshua 3:5 NIV) To consecrate means to "dedicate" yourself to the one who has created your life to be a masterpiece,

His masterpiece. The moment you choose to pick up the brush and paint the canvas of your life is the moment you skew the masterpiece. Imagine taking the Mona Lisa to a kindergarten art class perfecting their finger painting skills and giving them free reign to fix or paint as they see fit. Da Vinci's masterpiece—his dream, all his years of work—would be ruined in a moment. The palette must always yield to the artist.

Paul teaches in Romans 6:13: "Do not let any part of your body become an instrument of evil to serve sin. Instead, give yourselves completely to God, for you were dead, but now you have new life. So use your whole body as an instrument to do what is right for the glory of God." Yield to the master artist through daily obedience.

I celebrate church and love being able to speak about God, sharing His love and His Word with people on a weekly basis. I believe wholeheartedly what the writer of Hebrews champions in Hebrews 10:25: "And let us not neglect our meeting together, as some people do, but encourage one another, especially now that the day of his return is drawing near." To live fully as the masterpiece God desires you to be, you must go far beyond the minimal once-a-week experience where you depend on your pastor to get you through another week. That time of worship will add value to your spiritual life. But it's the things you do every day on a consistent basis that determine whether or not you succeed or fail—whether or not you live as a masterpiece or a forgery.

Results: success and victory!

As you make D.A.I.L.Y. consistency a part of your Life Palette, you pave the way for God to paint your life canvas with victory. In the story of Joshua and the children of Israel, we see it on the seventh day after the seventh time around the city. They did as God instructed, then, "when the people heard the sound of the rams' horns, they shouted as loud as they could. Suddenly, the walls of Jericho collapsed, and the Israelites charged straight into the town and captured it." (Joshua 6:20) It was success—but not without the consistency of what was needed daily to lead up to that moment.

After I spoke on this subject a few years ago, a lady in our church who was a nurse made an appointment to see me in my office. Through her tears, she shared how she had a dream, but felt she let it die because she wanted to please her mother. She never wanted to be a nurse. Over the next few months, she quit her job and went back to school to be a veterinarian. It had always been her dream to run an animal rescue shelter, and she realized it wasn't too late!

There are times in life when opportunities for fulfilling a dream have come and gone. The young athlete who wants to be a professional baseball pitcher and blows out his rotator cuff sees the years pass and, at some point, needs a new dream. While many exclaim God gives second chances, it's more accurate to say God gives new *opportunities*. Most of life does not allow for second chances, but God is the God of new opportunities because He desires for us to become the masterpieces He created us to be. Begin to seek God about the new opportunities He has for you. He'll always, until your dying breath, give you opportunities to live as a masterpiece.

> **While many exclaim God gives second chances, it's more accurate to say God gives new opportunities.**

Every day of your life, God is dipping into the colors of your Life Palette to apply brush strokes to your life canvas. The more you give Him a consistent palette to use, the more your life will look like the masterpiece He desires.

As great artists develop their palette, they tend to make careful choices of the colors they place on their palette. They typically lay out their palette in the same way each time so that reaching for a color becomes an unconscious decision, and the mixing of colors becomes a joy. It's true that artists will add or subtract colors to improve their palette, much the same way we add and subtract things as we grow in our life journey. Next, you'll learn how the discipline of living with a limited palette will improve your Life Palette more than anything else.

Palette Points

A fulfilled dream takes time. The dream God has given you will not be fulfilled in one day. Consistently move toward that dream daily.

1. What do you dream about? Not daydream, but are truly passionate about? Get out a pen and paper and write it down. Don't be afraid.

2. What one thing can you do today to advance one step forward toward the dream God has given you?

3. Do you initiate or procrastinate? Choose right now to be an initiator.

4. As God's masterpiece, it is important you are always learning and growing. Determine to be a lifetime learner. What area of your life do you need to learn more about to see the dream God has given you fulfilled?

My One Priority regarding consistency on my Life Palette:

Action Plan:

Chapter Nine

Keeping a Limited Palette

You've heard the phrase, "Jack of all trades, and master of none." For most people, that's how they live their lives. Yet trying to be good at many things will cause you to miss out on being great. The reality is you can't do it all, nor should you want to. Instead, as you focus on doing and being what God has created you to accomplish and become, you'll discover that living in your strengths is ultimately the most fulfilling way to live.

Your Life Palette is unique to God's desired masterpiece for you. Therefore, it's best to limit the focus of what you allow on your Life Palette. Most novice artists will start out with a very broad palette. When they see a color they want, instead of mixing it they'll go to the store and buy a tube of that color. As an artist improves, fewer colors are necessary on the palette. The fewer the colors, the more limited the palette becomes and the better the painting will be. My friend Phil Starke is a very successful artist, and for most of his career he has used a limited palette. He simply uses the primary colors of red, blue, and yellow, plus white and nothing else. Every color in the universe can be mixed from those three primary colors, and Phil is a master at being able to create the colors he wants from this limited palette.

The greatest secret to improving your Life Palette is developing the discipline of keeping and guarding a limited palette. The reason is simple: you have a limited amount of time, no matter how long you think you're going to live, and you're born with certain talents that are natural—plus a limited amount of abilities to supplement those talents. There's nothing more detrimental than getting distracted from living with a focus of developing these abilities and making the most of the time you are given.

A friend once told me the way to be most successful in life was to work on your weaknesses and turn them into strengths. Nothing could be further from the truth. God has given you natural strengths, but with those come natural weaknesses. How foolish it is to focus on your weaknesses, spending time trying to perfect something you're not good at, at the expense of ignoring further development of your natural strengths.

"Operation Log Roll"

When I was younger I used to do a lot of songwriting. I especially loved writing musicals. I wrote an Easter musical that was under contract with a music publisher out of Nashville and accepted by one of the top arrangers at the time. At one point, he asked me to rewrite a couple of the songs to make the musical stronger. I remember telling him how difficult I thought that would be—and I'll never forget what he told me: "Jeff, you're so natural that this will be like rolling off of a log." I went home, got out my music folder, and wrote in bold letters on the cover, "Operation Log Roll." That simple exhortation from the arranger changed my life, because it made me realize I was oblivious to my strongest abilities, the ones that came most natural to me. Since that time, I've noticed most people are like that: they don't recognize their own strengths. They know they're good at something, but they don't necessarily see it as a God-given strength.

Between the Palette Scrapings with Phil Starke

Primary colors are the foundation for color. Every other color is a modifier; they are all peripheral. Too many colors on a palette will make things muddy.

Whatever God has gifted you to do, you'll do it naturally—but because it seems so natural, there's also a tendency to feel like anybody could do it. When I first started speaking publicly, I thought everybody wanted to stand on a stage and speak to a crowd. It came as natural to me as sitting in my living room watching a football game; it wasn't something I had to make myself do. I didn't realize, though, that my ability to be in front of people and remain calm and comfortable was a natural gift until the day I hired a children's pastor who told me she would do anything I asked of her—except to get in front of a crowd and speak. I couldn't believe it. I thought everybody wanted to be the center of attention.

My problem was I often tried to work on my weaknesses, especially in areas of leadership where I needed to do things I really didn't enjoy doing. The more I labored with my weaknesses, the more frustrated I became, and at the same time the talents God had naturally given me were going unused. It was as though I was trying to add colors to my Life Palette God never intended to use on my life canvas, while removing the colors He wanted to use and limiting Him from painting His masterpiece.

A FEW TALENTS, A FEW OPPORTUNITIES, A FEW DAYS

In Matthew 25, Jesus gives us a trio of parables to teach about how we are to be vigilant with the gifts He has given us. He wants us to be faithful with our talents so we can be ready for His return and live effectively until He comes. The parables Christ uses shows us the necessity of focusing on a limited palette.

First, He uses the story of the bridesmaids, where He clearly teaches we are responsible to guard and protect our personal spiritual condition. Next, Christ tells the story of the talents, showing the importance of cultivating and using what He has entrusted to us. Finally, the story of the sheep and goats illustrates how serving others is a vital part of our limited palette.

In the parable of the talents, Jesus is not talking about earning salvation. It is a free gift from God, received only by His grace. What He is doing is providing an example of how to live in a rich and satisfying way (John 10:10). He tells of a man going on a long trip. The man gets his servants together and gives each of them different amounts of money to take care of while he's away. The word used here for "talents" is the Greek word *talanton*, which represents any kind of resource God gives us. The man then divides the talents in proportion to each servant's abilities. One servant receives five talents, the second servant two talents, and the third receives one talent. Each was given only what was needed to fulfill his responsibility. In the same way, each of us is given unique talents and abilities—but only what we need to fulfill His desires for our lives.

> **Whatever God has gifted you to do, you'll do it naturally—but because it seems so natural, there's also a tendency to feel like anybody could do it.**

If you're someone who does not yet recognize the talents you possess, it's vital you discover them. If you feel like God hasn't given you any talents, that's simply not true. Take some time with someone who knows and loves you, and ask them to describe what they see as your strengths and gifts. There are also many great resources to help you identify your talents, such as spiritual gift and personality tests. Just have no doubt: God has given you talents that you're responsible to cultivate—and the parable of the talents gives you three essentials on how to be vigilant in developing them in your life.

Essential #1: Be faithful. When the man returned, he came back to settle his accounts. He discovered the first servant had doubled his talents, as had the second servant. His response to them was immediate and positive: "Well done, my good and faithful servant. You have been faithful in handling this small amount, so now I will give you many more responsibilities." (Matthew 25:21) He was full of praise and wanted to give each servant more responsibility. Why? Because they were faithful in handling the unique amount he'd given them. So many times we look at others and say, "I want their talents. I want their gifts.

I want their skills." In other words, we're saying to God we want to choose what *we* think we're gifted at doing—instead of developing what *He* knows we're best at doing. Yet God is the artist. (More on the third servant later.)

While faithfulness is not necessarily in vogue in our culture, it is crucial for your Life Palette and for masterpiece living. In a day and time when we are often convinced we're entitled to what we have, we can easily miss the necessity of being faithful with all God has given us. Faithfulness is a value that's never out of vogue in God's kingdom and one He will always honor: "If you are faithful in little things, you will be faithful in large ones. But if you are dishonest in little things, you won't be honest with greater responsibilities. And if you are untrustworthy about worldly wealth, who will trust you with the true riches of heaven? And if you are not faithful with other people's things, why should you be trusted with things of your own?" (Luke 16:10-12)

Essential #2: Have focus. Most great Bible characters are known for having done one thing. Noah built the ark. David killed Goliath. Moses parted the Red Sea. People who are truly competent and successful, living their lives as the masterpiece God created them to be, have learned to focus on the few talents God has given them. They have a limited palette that comes from having a narrow focus.

My son and I love to go target shooting. For us, taking our shotguns out into the desert and blasting clay pigeons is a perfect day. Now, imagine two clay pigeon targets. One is hit with a shotgun loaded with pellet shells, and not a single BB from the shell hit the center of the target; the other is hit with a bullet from a rifle, right through the bull's eye. Unlike the first target littered with holes but none that hit the middle, the second target had one hole where the bullet struck true. The bull's eye hit illustrates the importance of focusing your time, talents, and treasure on your Life Palette. Without a narrow focus, you may hit the target but never hit the bull's eye. With the single focus of a limited palette, you'll become the masterpiece God created you to be.

Essential #3: Be diligent. Many artists never work with a limited palette because they never learned how to mix colors from the primaries.

Instead, they're dependent on a paint company mixing a color and selling it to them in a tube. They haven't been diligent in learning how to mix color. Don't look for the quick and easy way when it comes to developing your talents. Nothing is sadder than to arrive at an opportunity God has given you, only to find yourself ill-equipped to use your strengths because you took shortcuts rather than being diligent.

> **Without a narrow focus, you may hit the target but never hit the bull's eye.**

That brings us back to the third servant who buried his talent, not using faithfulness, focus, or diligence. "To those who use well what they are given, even more will be given, and they will have an abundance. But from those who do nothing, even what little they have will be taken away. Now throw this useless servant into outer darkness, where there will be weeping and gnashing of teeth." (Matthew 25:29-30) The words Jesus uses in the parable may seem harsh, but note the man in the story refers to the unfaithful servant as "useless." None of us want to be a useless servant to our Lord.

I love to walk through graveyards and read the headstones. Graveyards are sad places—not because of death, but because of the many buried there who never became the masterpiece God created them to be. Such treks remind me to be vigilant with the few things, the few gifts, the few talents, and the few strengths God has given me. Imagine your loved ones someday reading your epitaph. What do you want them to read about you? I've often thought about having my headstone made up in advance and put in my office. Every day I could look at it and remember what I want others to think of me when I die.

Live like you were dying

One thing that cannot be a part of your limited palette is fear. Fear is the opposite of faith, and to live as a masterpiece is to live a life above fear. I've painted several versions of the painting "Fearless." The rock cropping is found in Sedona, Arizona, one of the favorite places my wife and I love to visit. I'm so drawn to paint that place and will probably return to it many more times because of how the rocks hang fearlessly over this canyon. It inspires faith.

A few years ago, Tim McGraw had a hit song called *Live Like You Were Dying*. I decided to do a five-week teaching series based on the song. During one of the creative sessions with my staff, they came up with the idea for me to go and experience everything in the song and capture it on video to serve as the introduction to each week's talk. The premise of the song is that a man discovers he is dying and is asked what he did once he found out the news. He responds that he went skydiving, Rocky Mountain climbing, and rode on a bull named Fu Manchu.

Between the Palette Scrapings with Phil Starke

When you have colors on your palette that shouldn't be there, they will keep you from harmonizing the colors of your painting.

I'm an adventurer and love to do things for the adrenaline rush. Still, filming these three things caused me to face a few of my fears. I'm not particularly fond of heights, and while flying in a plane has never bothered me, jumping out of one is a different story. As it turned out, it was not that hard, mostly because I was strapped to a professional parachutist. Right before we jumped I figured this would be my first and last leap, so I asked if we could do some flips before we opened the chute. We did and I would love to do it again.

I love being in the mountains, but going over the edge of a 400 foot cliff on the end of a rope was a new experience for me. Having a skilled instructor helped put my mind at ease, but hanging halfway down the cliff just to get the right camera angle was a bit harrowing. Still, I did it and enjoyed the experience.

Then came the bull riding. It was something I'd always fantasized trying, but I never thought I'd find someone who would actually allow me to ride a bull with no rodeo experience. I was wrong. One of my staff members found someone a few miles from my office who actually trains professional bull riders. When they told him what we were doing, he was willing to let me ride. My staff member immediately set the date and got the camera crew ready to go. When the day came and we arrived at the arena, I took a half-hour lesson and was told I was ready to go. I was also told the bull I'd be riding was for beginners. By the time it was my turn to ride, though, the trainer said all the beginner bulls had been ridden too much and needed a break. He told me I would instead ride one of the bulls used to train professionals, but he assured me it would be alright. When it took several cowboys to get the bull in the chute and ready to be ridden, I had my doubts. The animal was very agitated and twice the size of the beginner bulls.

The Lord desires courageous faith, the type of faith that births a willingness to act on what you believe.

Undeterred, I climbed on the bull's back like I knew what I was doing. As one of the cowboys pulled the rope tight on my hand, I muttered, "I think this is going to hurt." Then I acted like the cowboys I'd seen in rodeos on TV. I nodded my head and hollered, "Let's go boys!" They opened the shoot and the bull started bucking. I didn't make it the 2.7 seconds McGraw mentions in the song. That bull slammed me to the ground with a force I never thought possible. I had pictured myself falling off gracefully, but there was no falling to it. Instead, the bull had knocked me out, broken a few of my ribs, and given me a headache that lasted several days. I didn't feel like I was living like I was dying. I just felt like I was dying.

The videos were a hit with the congregation. More than that, I'd faced my fears and was able to speak with total integrity as I challenged others to do the same in their lives. Fear cannot be the factor that limits you from living in the strengths of your limited palette, yet it's easy to allow fear to paralyze you. So how do you break free from its influence?

1. Get people to help you. The skydiving instructor made it clear before the plane left the ground that once we got in the air, there was no backing out. The guys who tied me to the rope and sent me over the edge of the cliff are friends who are skilled rock climbers. They love me and wanted to keep me safe, so I knew I could trust them.

Having people in your life who know your strengths, believe in you, and won't accept anything less than your best is imperative. From the time I was a teenager, I've had mentors to help me on my journey. I pour myself into the lives of others when I mentor. As followers of Jesus, we should always be in the process of being trained and of giving training to other people; both are part of masterpiece living. Nothing will spur on your personal growth like taking what you've learned and teaching it to others.

2. When opportunities come, be prepared to strap on and go for the ride. I'll never go bull riding again, but I'm so glad I did it when I had a chance. It stretched me way beyond my ability and reminded me how much I love adventure. I still like the Tim McGraw song and the idea it communicates to make the most of every opportunity God gives us. I'm also reminded that being faithful, focused, and disciplined to have a limited palette does not mean you never take risks. The Lord desires *courageous* faith, the type of faith that births a willingness to act on what you believe—to risk, step out, and do what God is leading you to do.

James, the brother of Jesus, wrote this about boldly following through on your faith: "So you see, faith by itself isn't enough. Unless it produces good deeds, it is dead and useless." (James 2:17) We can't separate *having* faith from *applying* faith by action. As an artist, I paint with oil paint. In my use of a limited palette, I will sometimes introduce a new color just to keep things fresh. Often I find the color in my cabinet where I store the paint tubes I rarely use. Unused and old, the color pigment is often separated from the linseed oil found in oil paint. It's useless for painting until I mix the separated pigment once again with the linseed oil. Every time we separate faith from application, we render it useless on our Life Palette. To develop a limited palette that'll work, we must discern those areas of life where we are separating what we believe from what we are willing to act upon. Applied faith is courageous faith.

Knowing your talents, using them well, and having the fearless faith to follow through on what God is telling you to do will give you the limited palette necessary for masterpiece living. Sometimes, though, you also need the discernment and boldness to eliminate—or scrape away—those things from your life that undermine your ability to be everything God has created you to be. It may be painful, but it's necessary. Best of all, you're about to discover it's something God has equipped you to do.

Palette Points

Focusing on your strengths and gifts is imperative for living as a masterpiece. Consider limiting your palette. You will be less stressed and more energized.

1. Think back to when you were younger. What were the things that came naturally to you?

2. Do you feel you are living in your strengths today, or are you working to always compensate for weaknesses?

3. Masterpiece living requires you to be faithful in cultivating the strengths God has given you. Rate yourself in each of the three essentials necessary for developing your strengths:

    - Essential #1. Be Faithful
    - Essential #2. Have Focus
    - Essential #3. Be Diligent

4. Write an epitaph you hope your loved ones would put on your headstone.

My One Priority regarding a limited palette:

Action Plan:

Chapter Ten

The Importance of Scraping

After a trip to the Oregon coast, I painted "Rising Tide," a 36 by 36-inch piece. When asked how long it took to paint the scene on such a large canvas, I said the answer isn't that simple because of all the scraping, or removing of layers of paint, necessary to finish the piece. By the time I released "Rising Tide" to the public, I'd scraped and repainted it three times. Confident I was finally done; I posted a photo of it on Facebook and wrote a little about the experience of creating it. Many people responded, saying they loved it and thought it was a great piece.

Then I received the call from my friend and art mentor Phil Starke. He saw "Rising Tide" online and offered a few suggestions to improve the piece. My first reaction was that I was done. I'd already repainted most of the canvas three times. Besides, after all that hard work and brush mileage, I was getting a great response from people who followed my work. My wife Kathy, who markets all of my art, had already listed it for sale and even had some potential buyers.

"Rising Tide" sat on an easel in the corner of my studio over the next week-and-a-half while I started working on several other pieces at my main easel. Every time I looked at it, I was reminded of Phil's encouragement to improve it. At first, I refused to allow myself to see what he was saying, simply because I wanted to be done—and, truth be told, I can sometimes get a little defensive about my work. But with each passing day, I found myself seeing more and more what he was seeing, and thinking how much better the painting would be if I reworked it according to Phil's suggestions.

I held out one more day, and then couldn't stand it any longer. I told Kathy to take "Rising Tide" off the market and I got to work scraping and repainting nearly the entire canvas once more, leaving only the sky untouched. I spent another day reworking and repainting the piece, incorporating the things Phil challenged me to consider. The end result was a much improved painting and, as an artist, I was much more satisfied.

Between the Palette Scrapings with Phil Starke

Don't be afraid to scrape your canvas to make the painting better. The problem for most artists is we fall in love with a color or a brush stroke, then we paint around it instead of removing it.

God's not finished with you yet

Perhaps you've seen the popular bumper sticker that says, "God's not finished with me yet." I find that statement to be trite but true and, when fully understood and accepted, profound. To know and understand that God is still working on the canvas of my life so I can fully reflect Him as the artist, is to acknowledge that just when I feel like I'm doing pretty good, He begins scraping and repainting. He begins improving.

As an artist who has envisioned His masterpiece from the first brush stroke of life to the last, God is not willing to leave anything on the canvas that's different from what He intended. He won't leave anything undone or accept something that's wrong and distracting from the overall masterpiece. He has a final picture in mind, and while we may not fully see it or understand, God as the artist clearly sees His desired end result. "Dear friends, we are already God's children, but he has not yet shown us what we will be like when Christ appears. But we do know that we will be like him, for we will see him as he really is." (1 John 3:2)

"God's not finished with me yet?" He's not. Yet the idea that He's working *on,* or better stated, *in* me conjures up all kinds of painful images, such as a dentist's chair. While my dentist is a dear personal friend and my checkups are mostly pain free, I still get tense when I sit in his chair. I know he has my best in mind, and that his work will improve my health and likely prevent future pain, but I hate the sound of the drill and the smells and…well, you get the picture. Still, I choose to trust my dentist.

In the same way, when God works, our trust in Him is put to the test. I often tell Him, "Father, this feels painful. This is not what I had in mind when I was praying for your will to be done." Or, "Jesus, when you said that you came to give me abundant life, I pictured something far more pain free. Why is that drill in your hand?" When God takes the knife to the canvas of my life and begins scraping, I'm challenged anew to trust Him.

In his book *Alla Prima*, Richard Schmid tells fellow artists to "never knowingly leave anything wrong on your canvas." If that's true for an artist like me who is creating works that will eventually vanish and deteriorate, how much more true is it for God as the master artist of my life who is creating His masterpiece that'll last forever?

It's not His fault

Logically, it's easy to argue, "God, if you're the artist and the one putting brush strokes on my life canvas, and then you decide it needs scraping, why should I be the one to suffer the consequences? I can't help it if you are less than perfect when it comes to painting my life as a masterpiece. That's your fault." It may sound preposterous, but you've probably had a moment when you thought, "I wish God had painted it right the first time." That's when you must remember again that your role is to develop your Life Palette. Up until the moment you had that thought, God was limited by the values, the attitudes, and the inconsistencies you gave Him to work with on your palette. Yet He gives you the ability and passion to place the right things on your Life Palette for Him to paint a masterpiece. "For God is working in you, giving you the desire and the power to do what pleases him." (Philippians 2:13)

As the artist, God is never to blame. He is perfect in all He is and does. If there's something wrong with the masterpiece of your life, you need to look at other causes—and chances are pretty good God has already been speaking to you about them. Perhaps you have something on your Life Palette that's not supposed to be there. It may be a value that doesn't line up with His values found in the Bible, or it may be your perspective or attitude is not in alignment with His.

God as the artist clearly sees His desired end result.

Artists often talk about how a painting gets "muddy." The colors are graying, they're not crisp and brilliant, or they seem to all run together. Sometimes the problem is that the artist keeps reworking the painting without scraping off the old paint, thus mixing in new and different colors with every brush stroke. Other times the artist simply never takes time to clean the brush or palette and the colors get mixed unintentionally. The best scraping always begins on the palette. The cleaner the palette, the less likely anything is going to get in the mix and mess up the painting on the canvas. When there are things on your Life Palette that shouldn't be there, they'll always be a part of the mix available to God. Eventually, He will have to scrape it off to get the result He has in mind. In the meantime, He's waiting for you to get those incorrect things off your Life Palette so He can take the painting of your life to a new level of masterpiece living. It's simply a process of elimination: check your values, your attitude, your character—all aspects of your Life Palette—to ensure you're developing and maintaining a good, clean palette.

Another possibility is that you're leaving something off your Life Palette that actually needs to be there. You discover you have some values that align with God and His Word, but maybe there are others you don't think are quite ready to make the palette. Let's say you value loving and having a relationship with God, yet you don't want to have to love others in the way Jesus did. "Jesus replied, 'You must love the LORD your God with all your heart, all your soul, and all your mind.' This is the first and greatest commandment. A second is equally important: 'Love your neighbor as yourself.' The entire law and all the demands of the prophets are based on these two commandments." (Matthew 22:37-40) In this case, God the artist surely would've already used the value of "wanting to love God" to begin to paint the masterpiece of your life, but because the value "loving others" is missing, He'll continually work to correct that, often through scraping. It's painful, but it's necessary to improve the masterpiece.

Why not just paint over?

In art workshops, scraping is something most teachers have to prod their students to do; most students, especially the novices, resist. They simply don't want to scrape off all the work (and lose all the hours) they've already put on the canvas. Instead, they want to keep working with what's bad and make it good. All that does is make things worse. Think about how muddy your life is when you try to mix your own, often sinful, values with the values of God? It just doesn't work.

In most of the workshops I've attended, the instructor will eventually hear the sound of someone taking out their palette knife and scraping their canvas to repaint a section, and I'll hear the teacher say, "That is a sweet sound." Why? Because they know it is a mature and right thing to do; that the artist cares too much to settle for poor work. Yet why can't an artist just paint over what's already painted on the canvas? Not only will the painting have a dull appearance, but something even worse could happen: a section you covered up could reappear.

Ghost horse

I once sold a collector a painting of a horse in a pasture. It had been on my drying rack for several months while waiting to be sold and I hadn't looked at it in all that time. When Kathy went to ship it, she brought the painting to me, saying there was a problem I was going to have to deal with immediately before she could send the painting to the collector.

What happened? In the original painting there were two horses in the pasture. As I worked on the composition I felt it was much stronger with the focus on just one horse, so I painted over the second horse instead of scraping it off. Now the second horse was reappearing through the top layer of paint, looking like a ghost. The painting was sold, the collector was expecting shipment, and there was no easy fix. After many hours of scraping and repainting, the ghost horse was exorcized; however, if I'd taken a moment to scrape it away in the first place, I would've saved myself a ton of time and effort. Even after reworking that painting, I'm still afraid someday I'll get a call from the collector telling me that he suddenly has another horse appearing in the painting.

It is much better to have a sin or mistakes in your life removed than covered up. Titus 3:4-5 tell us, "When God our Savior revealed his kindness and love, he saved us, not because of the righteous things we had done, but because of his mercy. He washed away our sins, giving us a new birth and new life through the Holy Spirit." This passage paints a picture of God as the artist scraping the canvas of your life—not simply covering up what was already there, but removing it altogether so that it'll never reappear. That's how God works. He doesn't want you to live haunted by the potential of the past resurfacing, so He scrapes the canvas and reworks it. Unfortunately, this is often held at bay until you pause and rework your Life Palette.

Taking a chocolate break

I've painted in a couple of workshops presented by artist Jim Wilcox. On the syllabus for his workshops, Jim identifies the colors of paint to use, the brushes he wants you to have—and he insists that you bring chocolate. Throughout the day, he schedules chocolate breaks for the entire class. No one is exempt. Sure, Jim loves chocolate, but it's inclusion on the syllabus is also a reminder that as an artist you need to stop, stand back, and look at what you are painting. If you never do this, you can be painting wrong values or bad composition and never know it until you're done, making the rework more difficult, if not impossible.

Hopefully, you've already made some changes to your Life Palette, or at least have a working list for improvement. So how can you protect and continue to improve your Life Palette the rest of your life? It's vital to have a simple action plan to take "chocolate breaks" on a regular basis when it comes to making sure your Life Palette is always ready for the master to paint.

Action #1: Encounter God daily. Set aside time to spend with the one who is painting the masterpiece of your life. Have a daily encounter with Him. This involves so much more than reading a Bible verse or two and saying a quick prayer asking Him to bless your day. This needs to be a time when you utilize study, prayer, and worship to really look at the key elements of your Life Palette.

It is much better to have a sin or mistakes in your life removed than covered up.

Action #2: Evaluate. Purposefully look at your values, attitudes, character, and other elements, asking God to guide you in how you can be more like Him and live in a way that'll better reflect Him. Artists often look into a mirror to evaluate their painting. There's something about looking at your canvas in reverse that helps you see what's working and what's not. You can do the same with your Life Palette. I love the way Eugene Peterson writes David's prayer of evaluation in Psalm 139:23-24 in The Message: "Investigate my life, O God, find out everything about me; Cross-examine and test me, get a clear picture of what I'm about; See for yourself whether I've done anything wrong—then guide me on the road to eternal life." Make that your prayer as you evaluate your Life Palette during your daily encounter with God.

Action #3: Eliminate. Get rid of those things you see on your Life Palette that should no longer be there—and do it immediately. There's never a good reason to put it off, so ask God to empower you to have the self-control to deal with these issues right away. Anything wrong that is not eliminated quickly will make its way to the canvas. Left unchecked for several days or weeks, something that shouldn't be on your Life Palette

Life Palette

will contaminate other areas. A value that is even a little off will affect your perspective and your attitude, and before you know it a major overhaul will be needed rather than a simpler, daily adjustment. In Matthew 6:11, Jesus taught His disciples to pray, "Give us today…" revealing the necessity of encountering, evaluating, and eliminating daily.

Getting it right

In the times I painted with Jim Wilcox, I can't tell you how often he would stand behind me, point out something wrong, and tell me I needed to take my palette knife, scrape it, and paint it again. Often I wouldn't want to scrape and at times was fearful I couldn't repaint it better. Jim always responded the same way: "Jeff, you painted it once. You can paint it again. Get it right!"

I've identified **four common causes to mediocrity** on your Life Palette—things that cause you to settle for what you have instead of adjusting, scraping, and getting it right. It's important you see them and understand, with His help, that you can scrape them off your Life Palette so the master artist can paint your life to be all He created it to be.

Between the Palette Scrapings with Phil Starke

If the values are wrong, you have to scrape it. If the composition is off, you have to scrape it. Always be willing to change your painting to make it right—to make it a masterpiece.

---

1. Faking it

Often we fake our way though things because we're simply not willing to pay the price to do it right. Although my wife Kathy doesn't paint, she's developed quite an eye for art. It's amazing how many times there's been an area of a painting that I can't get right—and I try to fake my way through addressing it—she will invariably spot it.

Be honest. There are areas essential for your Life Palette where you know you're just getting by. Whatever the reasoning—you don't think you have what it takes to change or that the thing is simply a part of who you are—you try to fake it. Perhaps it's a character flaw you've faked your way through for years, but you know it's holding you back. God can only work with the palette you give Him. Eventually that flaw will reveal itself on the canvas of your life.

Of course, it's easy to see these shortcomings in the lives of others. For example, when you think of Richard Nixon, what's the first thing that comes to mind? Even if you're poor at history, it's probably the Watergate scandal. Nixon gave his life to public service and accomplished many great achievements over the course of his political career, but a legacy of trusted character was erased by one thing. It's as if you walked up to the Mona Lisa and put one big red brush stroke across her face. Suddenly that's all you see. You no longer notice the masterpiece beneath.

Whatever area of your Life Palette you're faking, do what's necessary to become authentic in that area. Admit it to yourself and to God. Prayerfully ask for His power and help. Find someone you trust who can mentor you and lead you to a new level in that area. Then make sure you don't "fake the fix." It may take time and struggle to transform to what is truly needed on your Life Palette, but commit to do the work. No shortcuts allowed.

2. Not enough time

People tell me all the time they don't have enough time to do what they want to do or, more importantly, what they sense God wants them to do. But it's almost never an issue of time; rather, it's one of choices and priorities. Truth is, God has given you plenty of time to do and be what He created you to do and be. If you feel you need more than 24 hours in a day, then you are either doing something God did not create you to do, or you're doing what He wants but without developing the skills to accomplish it more efficiently.

A friend told me about a professor he had in a college painting class who always told his class to use more paint. Most beginning artists want to conserve paint, especially when they realize how much good paint costs. The professor would pick up a student's tube of paint, squeeze the entire contents from the tube onto their palette, and tell them to use it all on the canvas. God has given you all the time you need to be His masterpiece and He's telling you to use it all! During your daily encounter with God, evaluate the time wasting activities in your life and work to eliminate them.

3. Doing things right

You've likely heard the saying, "If it's worth doing, it's worth doing right." Scrape that idea from your Life Palette, because a need for perfectionism will keep you from doing anything at all. Instead, say this: "If it's worth doing, it's worth doing wrong." You are not God. You're not going to get everything right the first time, so accept there will be some scraping involved. Masterpieces require doing it wrong, scraping, and doing it again.

4. Shadows

To the novice eye, the shadows of paintings are simply dark shades. Yet one of the ways you can tell how well someone is painting is by seeing what they paint in the shadows. You may not see it at first, but the next time you see an original painting that captivates you, get in closer and look at how the artist painted the shadows. When most great artists paint shadows, they are full of rich color. Carl Runguis is one of my favorite artists whose pieces come to life because of what he places in the shadows.

Everyone has painful things from their past. These hurts can become shadows in our lives that cause us to hide and prevent us from expressing our lives as masterpieces. While I'd never say God creates all the pain in our lives, I do believe that He will never waste a painful moment. "And we know that God causes everything to work together for the good of those who love God and are called according to his purpose for them." (Romans 8:28) There's plenty about that verse I

LIFE PALETTE

Rosebud Falls
30 x 24"
Location: Rosebud Falls, Montana (Commission)

Sedona First Impression
9 x 12"
Location: Sedona, Arizona, *en plein air*

To view or purchase Jeff's art, check out www.jeffloveart.com   Q

Life Palette

Simply Sky
18 x 24"
Location: Eastern Colorado

Sky Dance
24 x 36"
Location: Old Marana, Arizona

LIFE PALETTE

Summer Color Show
24 x 30"
Location: Old Marana, Arizona

Summer On The Western Lowlands
24 x 48"
Location: Wyoming Teton Mountains

Life Palette

The Gentle Roll
30 x 40"
Location: Beach In Maui, Hawaii

The Road To Remember
18 x 24"
Location: Country road in central Oregon

Towering Teewinot
30 x 24"
Location: Grand Teton National Park

To view or purchase Jeff's art, check out www.jeffloveart.com

don't understand. What I do know is that for the sake of living your life as a masterpiece, every area where you have experienced pain is a place God wants to use to create a better masterpiece. It's interesting to note that in oil painting, you typically start with the dark colors first. Everything else is painted in relationship to the colors in the shadows. That's true of life as well. A person who has never experienced the shadows, the darkness of life, has not yet been tested or tried. Those who have, and in turn have allowed God to paint His life and love into their shadows, have a masterpiece quality about them.

> **Say this: "If it's worth doing, it's worth doing wrong."**

Embracing the process

As an artist, I thoroughly enjoy the entire process of painting. As the artist of your life, God enjoys creating and developing your life into a masterpiece. He is bound only by what you place or allow on your Life Palette. Be willing to scrape your palette clean on a regular basis and guard it. The fact that God is willing to scrape your life canvas is not a reflection of His failure or limitation, but a picture of your potential and growth as His masterpiece.

I'm writing this in my studio with the painting "Rising Tide" hanging on the wall directly in front of me. I'm starting to think there might be some areas that again need to be scraped and repainted. It can still be improved! There is, however, a big difference between improving a painting and simply changing a painting. When an artist changes things without knowing the "why" behind the change, it can often end in disaster. Next, we're going to look at one thing that *never* needs to change on your Life Palette for masterpiece living.

Palette Points

Most of us don't like it when God begins to scrape away something in our lives. He has created you as a masterpiece and desires nothing less. Are there things on your Life Palette you know should *not* be there? Are there things you know need to *be* there?

1. What elements are part of your Life Palette that you know "muddy up" your life as God's masterpiece? Be honest and write them down. What do you need to do to get them off your Life Palette?

2. What elements *missing* from your Life Palette are keeping you from living as God's masterpiece? Prayerfully consider this. Ask God to direct you.

3. Which of these need the most focus to clean your Life Palette and keep it clean?

   - Encounter God daily
   - Evaluate daily
   - Eliminate daily

4. Look back at the four causes of mediocrity and make sure none of them are on your Life Palette.

   - Faking it
   - Not enough time
   - Doing things right
   - Shadows

My One Priority for scraping my Life Palette:

Action Plan:

Chapter Eleven

Chasing the Light

Everything in a painting is affected by light—and every masterpiece has a predominate light source. As an artist begins to paint, he must reach conclusions regarding that light source, as well as the importance of having an established source of light.

If that reads a little like double talk, let me clarify. In the art world, especially for artists who paint *en plein air* (French for "painting outside"), there is a well-worn phrase that's never used as a positive: "chasing the light." It means you keep changing the painting to keep up with the movement of the sunlight. The shadows change and the areas that have light illuminating them change, so you feel you must keep changing the painting. It doesn't take a rocket scientist to understand that if you paint by that motto, you'll never complete a painting because you'll constantly start over. While it's important to scrape and repaint, chasing the light is not a matter of scraping. It's a matter of a *steady* light source.

"Arroyo Rosa" was a piece I painted in my studio. I knew the sun was about to set and I would not be able to capture the light I wanted before it became dark. To capture such a moment of beauty on canvas, I therefore made the light source steady by taking as many photographs as I could at the moment the light was just right. I do, however, love the challenge of painting sunsets *en plein air*. It helps me paint fast and free because I know my light source is moving quickly.

Every life has a steady light source, too. For some, it is self; for many, it is their culture or other people; for others still, it may be the whims of the moment. Living with a predominate light source that's unsteady or always moving will always result in a life lived as a forgery—or worse, one that is unfinished, never going forward because of repeated restarts.

STICKING WITH IT

So how does an artist successfully paint outside since the sunlight is always moving? He makes a decision about the light source, sticks with it for the shadows and colors, and then paints fast. The artist will ask himself several questions to inform his decision. Where is the light source coming from? What is the temperature of the main light source and how will it affect the painting? How is the light affecting the shadows and shade? What is the darkest dark and lightest light that are being reflected in the painting as a result of the light source?

God is not only the artist painting the masterpiece of your life—God Himself *is* light. Jesus said it this way: "I am the light of the world. If you follow me, you won't have to walk in darkness, because you will have the light that leads to life." (John 8:12) Notice that we do not create light for our lives as masterpieces; we are not the source of light. Instead, Christ declares He is the source of light for all living things. As we follow Him, we *reflect* Him as the light that illuminates our lives as His masterpiece.

REFLECTING LIGHT

Like us, the paint—the colors and pigments an artist carefully places on a canvas to create the masterpiece he desires—has no ability to create light. It merely reflects whatever light source is available to illuminate it. If you're not sure about that, just turn off the lights in the room you're in and look at any picture hanging on the wall. Without the light, you quickly see how the colors in the pictures change. If you're completely in the dark, the colors of the painting appear dark. In the middle of the afternoon, you may have light from the sun coming through your windows and reflecting off the walls and floor, so the colors of the painting are not as dark, but reflect the added amount of light available.

While God Himself is the source of light and the artist of our lives as His masterpiece, He has also given us the freedom to *choose* for our

Life Palette the light source that our masterpiece will reflect. Consider Jesus' words in Matthew 5:14-16: "You are the light of the world—like a city on a hilltop that cannot be hidden. No one lights a lamp and then puts it under a basket. Instead, a lamp is placed on a stand, where it gives light to everyone in the house. In the same way, let your good deeds shine out for all to see, so that everyone will praise your heavenly Father." Yet Jesus also calls Himself the light of the world. Is He confused? He says He's the light of the world and that we are the light of the world. Which one is it? The context of our lives as a masterpiece makes it clear. Throughout Scripture we see God as the light source and we are created and intended to be reflections of His light. Paul states: "So all of us who have had that veil removed can see and reflect the glory of the Lord." (2 Corinthians 3:18)

Light that leads to masterpiece living

Colors are the color they are because of pigment. Pigment simply absorbs certain spectrums of colors from its light source and does not absorb others. In other words, red is red because it only absorbs the red spectrum of light; therefore, we see it as red because it only reflects what it absorbs. But turn off the light source and red no longer is reflecting red. It may look dark blue, purple, or even jet black.

> **Every life has a steady light source.**

In the same way, our lives reflect the light source, be it the light of God or the forged light of the world. When we choose God as our light source, the canvas of our lives reflects a masterpiece. Jesus told us, "Your eye is a lamp that provides light for your body. When your eye is good, your whole body is filled with light. But when it is bad, your body is filled with darkness. Make sure that the light you think you have is not actually darkness. If you are filled with light, with no dark corners, then your whole life will be radiant, as though a floodlight were filling you with light." (Luke 11:34-36) With the right light source, our whole life is radiant; God as our light source is reflected on our life canvas, so Jesus warns us to be sure our light source is not darkness, but His true light.

In his book Alla Prima, author and artist Richard Schmid says "color is to seeing what flavor is to eating." Color is what brings a masterpiece to life. It's what makes one painting stand out from another. Yet the number one thing I hear artists talk about is problems with color—and how light affects the colors in their paintings. Why? They don't understand the behavior of color as it relates to reflecting the light source. Light does not simply lighten or darken a color on a canvas, it *changes* the color. The light source of your life does not simply diminish or augment your life, it changes it because your life is reflecting whatever your light source is at that very moment.

There are four primary things you can do on your Life Palette to assure you have true light and that your life always reflects that light.

1. Choose God's Word as your light source

The Bible changes the colors of your life. Remember, an artist cannot duplicate light. The pigment of the paint simply reflects the light source. You cannot produce light on the canvas of your life, but you certainly reflect it. The choice you have on your Life Palette is, "Who or what is going to be my light source?" That choice determines what you expose yourself to and ultimately what your life reflects.

Jesus came and walked among humans as the living Word of God: "So the Word became human and made his home among us. He was full of unfailing love and faithfulness. And we have seen his glory, the glory of the Father's one and only Son." (John 1:14) As the living Word, Christ declared Himself to be the light of the world. Now you have the written Word as a way for you to absorb the light of God as your light source so you reflect His glory as His masterpiece. As you choose to follow Jesus, you do not have to walk in darkness; instead, you are walking in—that is, reflecting—His light in your life.

Make the commitment that the light source on your Life Palette is going to be the written Word of God. As you do this, it changes what your life canvas reflects because you're absorbing a different light and seeing life through a different colored lens. Living in the Southwestern United States in the Sonoran Desert, I don't see the brilliant greens that trees in the Midwest possess. The lack of rainfall and the sun's brilliance keeps me from seeing all those beautiful colors that I saw on a drive through the Ohio countryside where I grew up. Yet one day, while driving through the desert, my wife Kathy commented about how incredibly green the desert looked that day and commented how it must be because of the rain the day before. I didn't see what she was seeing, and suggested she take off her sunglasses and take another look. The lenses she was wearing made the colors of the desert look more vivid than they really were.

When you choose to make God's Word the lens your life is seen through, you will see and reflect His light exactly as He intended. It will transform you: "Don't copy the behavior and customs of this world, but let God transform you into a new person by changing the way you think. Then you will learn to know God's will for you, which is good and pleasing and perfect." (Romans 12:2) The psalmist adds in Psalm 119:105, "Your word is a lamp to guide my feet and a light for my path." When the Word of God lights the way for you to go in every step of your life, every color He has placed on the canvas of your life will always reflect Him and His light.

> **Every life reflects a light source.**

2. Develop a daily habit of exposure

Just as sure as the sun brings light with the dawn of each new day, you need to allow the written Word to enlighten your life each day. The power of this habit is the same as with any habit: you experience the results, good or bad, according to what that habit is. The exposure that you daily give your Life Palette to the truth of the Bible will bring many benefits to your life, not the least of which is knowledge about your salvation. "As you read what I have written," Paul states in Ephesians 3:4, "you will understand my insight into this plan regarding Christ."

For the sake of absorbing all of the light God wants your masterpiece to reflect, I encourage you to read the Bible systematically. Because

Life Palette

of the size of the entire Old and New Testament together, you may be intimidated and won't know where to start or what's most important for you to read. Often I hear stories of someone who resorted to the "hunt and peck" method: letting the pages of the Bible fly open, praying a quick prayer for God's guidance, and then sticking your finger down, hoping the verse it lands on is the one God wants to speak to you at that particular moment. While you may have had a time or two where that worked, it's not a method that'll give you exposure to the full light of His Word. I once heard of a man who was dealing with depression and used the "hunt and peck" method to ask God to reveal Himself. The first try, his finger stopped on Matthew 27:5, which read, "Then Judas threw the silver coins down in the Temple and went out and hanged himself." The man thought, "Surely this is not the verse God has for me," so he decided to give it another shot. This time his finger landed on Luke 10:37: "Then Jesus said, 'Yes, now go and do the same.'"

Between the Palette Scrapings with Phil Starke

It's important to establish your light source before putting paint on the canvas. If you are not clear about your light source or are always changing your light source, the painting will get muddy.

Humor aside, the newer you are to reading God's Word, the longer you should simply read the New Testament. Read about Jesus, the light of the world. Expose yourself to His life more than anything else. Whatever you do, especially if you're just beginning masterpiece living as a Christian, don't treat the Bible like any other book and start at the beginning (Genesis). You're living in New Testament times, so that's where you should begin. Also, don't allow your zealousness to discourage you. I have talked to many people who were convinced this needed to be a daily habit in their lives, deciding to read for an hour a day, only to quit from discouragement because they rarely completed their full hour. Instead, read until you have something you feel God is speaking to you—an insight you need to absorb and truly consider how it applies to the context of your life. If you miss a few minutes or skip a day, pick up where you left off as soon as possible. Don't quit. If you've ever missed a meal, you probably didn't get discouraged and quit eating over your failure to eat every meal.

3. Begin to dedicate key verses to memory

As I paint with other artists, it's easy to spot those who have not studied and understood the color wheel. They are not able to put into practice the simple system that the color wheel teaches. Their lack of command of color keeps them from creating a good painting.

Your command—your understanding and recall ability—of the truths of God's Word affects your life as His masterpiece. Psalm 119:11 says, "I have hidden your word in my heart, that I might not sin against you." As I talk about Scripture memorization, men often give the immediate excuse, "I'm just not good at remembering things." The truth is you'll remember what's important to you. Many times the same man who says he's not good at remembering things can rattle off the stats from his favorite football or baseball team with no effort at all. Is that an indictment about men and sports? No, but it proves a point that remembering the Bible is (ahem) possible—and will add far more value to your Life Palette and your ability to live daily as the masterpiece God created you to be.

The more you dedicate key Scripture verses to memory, the more empowered you will be to resist temptations that will lead you toward darkness instead of light. When you face major decisions in your life, it's important to know and understand the wisdom of God so it can light your path. You will experience strength when you are in stressful situations and, more importantly, reflect His light in everything you do and say in those moments.

As you go about your day, the colors you see are already blended together with all they've absorbed from the light spectrum, and their beauty is reflected for you to experience. Artists, though, are trained to see colors differently and as they truly are, not how they appear at first glance. A novice painter looking at a mountainside full of trees will paint the trees green and wonder why it doesn't look right. The trained painter knows that even though the leaves on the trees are green, their true color in the distance may be more gray or dark blue. To go about life living by what you think you know—through culture, or from your past, or the way you were raised—is to assume every time you see a tree and want to paint it on the canvas, you paint it green. As you put the light of God's Word to memory, you will be getting the true color for every brush stoke God wants to paint on your life canvas.

4. Respond to the light

Phil Starke was once asked in an interview about the keys to painting successfully outside. He pointed out it was so important to "respond to the light." I asked Phil what he meant by that, and he explained an artist must understand how the light is changing the color of whatever it is he's painting, and then commit to painting his subject the way it is reflecting the light.

How true that is to live life as the masterpiece God intends. James the brother of Jesus said, "But don't just listen to God's word. You must do what it says. Otherwise, you are only fooling yourselves … if you do what it says and don't forget what you heard, then God will bless you for doing it." (James 1:22, 25) You can't just choose His Word as your light source and not put it into practice. You can't memorize a verse or two, or chapters for that matter, and think that you will suddenly begin to look like the masterpiece God created you to be. You must begin, in Phil's words, to respond to the light. Do what it says.

Rekeying a masterpiece

I once attended a workshop from an artist who was demonstrating how to rekey a painting and its importance. To "rekey" a painting simply means to bring the values and color to a lighter or darker level, depending on which direction the artist feels it needs to go. In my case, I tend to rekey a lot of my paintings to a brighter value; that is, to place within them a sense of more light because I have a tendency to key them darker than I should when I begin my paintings.

The light of God's Word will transform us or, in Life Palette jargon, rekey the painting on the canvas of our lives. Our masterpiece is painted and formed by the light of His Word as we respond to it. This is not a formula, because no formula can predict what life will bring today, much less tomorrow. This is about responding to the moment and allowing our lives to be exposed to His light regardless of what the moment brings. Light is the thing that brings balance and harmony to any painting and ultimately leads to a masterpiece.

Light to darkness

We've been learning under the premise of choosing what goes on our Life Palette. One of those things is to choose how to move from darkness to light. But it's amazing to recognize how quickly we can slip the other direction: from light to darkness. I was speaking at a church in Cincinnati, Ohio several years ago while staying with my mother and stepfather. As I walked out of the back of their house, I immediately stepped onto level ground in their backyard, but one side of the yard sloped off steeply to a lower level garage. One evening I went out back and, not being familiar enough with their yard to know where the slope began, I stepped out of the light into the darkness—and suddenly found myself tumbling down the hill toward the cement drive that led to the garage door. I gathered myself quickly; thankfully, only my pride was hurt as I got back up the hill. We are created to reflect the light of God. It is an imperative part of our Life Palette and vital to living successfully as His masterpiece. To knowingly live in the darkness and wonder why we stumble and fall, why our relationships fail, and why we never seem to make progress is like me stepping out of the light from their back porch and tumbling into the night.

> **With the right light source, our whole life is radiant.**

Life Palette

Every life reflects a light source. It is an incredible and terrible gift that God as an artist has placed in the hands of each of us. His desire is to paint the canvas of our lives every day and in every way to reflect Him, His glory, and His Word.

Letting His light dispel darkness

You may experience dark days when you're easily convinced your life is anything but a masterpiece. It's when you heard him say, "I'm leaving you," or when the doctor told you it was cancer. Perhaps on a lesser but still significant level, you've just had a tough year, or didn't get that promotion, or came to the realization that your hopes and dreams are never going to materialize.

Where is God and His light in all of that? How are you reflecting Him as a masterpiece during those moments? Be encouraged. God is where He's always been, right there with you. During the times that seem the hardest to navigate, make sure you are not chasing after one light source or another, trying to get a quick fix. This is when you need His Word most, knowing that your light source is a dependable, established source of truth.

Read Jesus' words again—this time slowly and carefully. Read them aloud: "I am the light of the world. If you follow me, you won't have to walk in darkness, because you will have the light that leads to life." (John 8:12) It's one thing to know there is a light source for your life, and that when you make it a part of your Life Palette, God will cause your life to reflect it as His masterpiece. It's quite another to clearly *choose* that source for all things, for all decisions, and for every path you take, determined to follow that light regardless of where it leads. You get to choose darkness or light. It's part of your Life Palette. Only His light will bring to life the colors God has placed on your life canvas.

As a masterpiece reflecting His light and, ultimately, His glory, it's imperative that you have the finishing touches that authenticate and frame it in a manner worthy of the master artist. Amazingly, God has already provided all that's needed to display a masterpiece. They are His finishing touches.

Palette Points

We are not the creators of light. We simply reflect it. We have the incredible privilege of choosing our light source and who or what we reflect. As you examine your Life Palette, consider the four primary things that will assure you have true light and will always reflect it.

1. What do you do in your life on a regular basis to assure God's Word is your light source? What changes do you need to make?

2. How can you make your daily habit of exposure more effective?

3. Develop a plan to dedicate key verses to memory. If this is new to you, start with one a week. Write it down, carry it with you, and say it over and over. You may want to begin with Psalm 119:11. Get an accountability partner who will do this with you.

4. Are you doing what you know to do from God's Word? Are there areas you need His help to change? Take a moment and pray about them. Ask Him to give you the strength you need. He wants to help you.

5. Are you a part of a Bible-teaching church to help you on this journey as a masterpiece? No, I mean *really*? Do you even know your pastor's name? If the church you attend is not teaching the Bible or is teaching something other than the Bible, change churches!

My One Priority regarding my light source:

Action Plan:

Chapter Twelve

The Finishing Touches

For artists, there's nothing quite like the day a painting is ready to leave the studio and go on display to the public. It's their masterpiece; they've labored over it with a purpose in mind and are excited to finally share it with the world. It's incredible for the artist to be at a gallery or a show and to hear the response of those who see the painting for the first time. "Isn't She Lovely" is one of those paintings I love to display. I've painted it several times—each one with a unique touch. It's a piece that I'm very proud of as an artist.

God the artist, your loving Heavenly Father, is also proud of you. He's excited about your life and how it reflects Him and all that He is. In His sovereignty, God sees and knows your past, present, and future. But here's an even more incredible truth. Because God is God, He has *already* added the finishing touches to the masterpiece of your life, even before it's completed. It's passionately inspired, personally signed, and carefully framed by Him. There's nothing more encouraging than to understand that God has already put the finishing touches on your life as His masterpiece. It brings you undeniable hope for the future! Yet as a real-life work of art, the display of your life as His masterpiece remains both limited and empowered by your Life Palette.

Let's look at the three finishing touches of a masterpiece. As you see how God has already labored over your life as the artist, you'll experience each in a fresh way every day and discover the power He gives to enable you to continually develop your Life Palette.

1. The *passion* touch

Any artist who has ever painted a masterpiece, be it in their own eyes or in the eyes of critics, will tell you it was birthed from a passionate pursuit burning within to paint the perfect painting. God has a passion, too, to see you live as the masterpiece He created you to be. Because of that passion, His love leads Him to cast out into the storms of your life, during times of your hopelessness, to find you and return you to the safety and warmth of His presence. It may be that you've drifted so far off the course of His design that His light seems like a small beacon on the horizon—so far away you can only hope it'll somehow find its way to you. However, if you will allow Him, He will come, rescue you, and lead you in the right direction.

Between the Palette Scrapings with Phil Starke

An artist's signature shows who created the piece. It authenticates it. The signature is the finishing touch of the composition.

God hasn't painted the canvas of your life to just leave you on your own to make the best of things. He has created you as His masterpiece with utmost skill and care: "You made all the delicate, inner parts of my body and knit me together in my mother's womb. Thank you for making me so wonderfully complex! Your workmanship is marvelous—how well I know it." (Psalm 139:13-14) Plus, God is doing everything in His power to get you to the place where you are living as His workmanship in the absolute assurance of the knowledge of who you are in Him, with the goal of being all He originally intended you to be. In 2 Corinthians 5:17, Paul declares that "anyone who belongs to Christ has become a new person. The old life is gone; a new life has begun!" "New person" in the original language means that you are recreated to the *original* design God created you to be. As the artist of your life, God will pursue you with His love and light to the very end of your life, passionately desiring for you to reflect the beauty of His handiwork as His masterpiece.

I'll never forget the first time I saw the Rocky Mountains. I was a teenager and had traveled with the youth group from our church in Ohio to a campground up in the mountains outside of Colorado Springs. As we were driving up the pass in the middle of the night I could see Pikes Peak in the moonlight. I was amazed and captivated with the Rocky Mountains from that moment on. When my family moved to Colorado Springs two years later, I began to pursue my passion for hiking in the Sangre de Cristo mountain range (Spanish for "The Blood of Christ") in southern Colorado, ultimately becoming a backpacking leader for youth groups who would visit from out of state. My goal was to ultimately hike all of the "fourteeners," mountains above 14,000 feet, of which there are 54 in Colorado alone.

> **He has created you as His masterpiece with utmost skill and care.**

In my early twenties, after getting married and moving to Texas to be a worship leader, I put together a group of men to periodically travel to that area to hike, climb, and fish. My plan for one particular trip was to fish for a few days with the guys, then climb to the top of a couple of the fourteeners the last day or two. I convinced one of the men, Jim, to join me for the climbs. Having had previous experience as a backpack leader, I was confident Jim and I could reach the summit and get back to camp in a single day.

When Jim and I set off for the first fourteener, there were several things going against us. First, I didn't tell the rest of the group which summit we would be going up that day. Second, there was a 13,000-foot peak we'd have to climb first, go back down in elevation, and then begin the ascent of the fourteener. Since we were camping just below tree line at about 12,000 feet, I didn't see this as a big deal. Third, I had not anticipated how non-acclimated I'd become to high altitude after a few short years living in the plains of Texas. To top it off, we'd have to do some bush whacking to reach the summit because there was no pre-existing trail from where we set up camp.

We set out that morning with vigor and full assurance that we were going to conquer Humboldt Peak. Not long after noon, Jim and I reached the summit and enjoyed the view for half an hour before beginning our descent. Typical for that time of year, an afternoon storm was blowing in so we knew we needed to hurry back to camp. We reached the valley floor and were ascending back up the 13,000-foot peak between us and camp when the storm suddenly hit and, before we knew it, the sun was setting. We knew we were in trouble. We got wet and began to get hypothermic. We could see the firelight from our camp a couple of miles down the mountainside, but in the dark could not see well enough to journey down. I knew from my training we needed to hunker down and take our chances out in the elements.

The storm intensified, and our only shelter was a rock formation; though we were tucked in beneath it as far as possible, it was not keeping us dry because of the slashing wind. As we hunched down in the dark of night, it was hard to maintain hope. I knew that even though it was July, it was still going to be a cold and dangerous night. We did the only thing we knew to do. We prayed.

To our amazement, we noticed the light from several flashlights bobbing their way away from our camp. We kept praying. We watched the others for several hours as they made decisions from one trail to another, all the while snaking straight up toward us. The hope birthed within me watching their flashlights dip up and down as they hiked toward us was remarkable. Once within shouting distance, they came right to us. Unknown to me, one of my other friends from the area had hiked that day to our camp to meet up with us. Because of his expertise in those mountains, he skillfully led the group of men to come and rescue us. They led us back to camp where we ate and got warm by the fire. The only lasting injury from the day was to my ego.

Many times since then I've pictured those dim flashlights leaving camp with fond recall of the hope that it gave us in our moment of hopelessness. It's a picture of how God so passionately pursues us when we are lost, hurting, disoriented, and alone in the darkness of life. He is making His way toward us in hot pursuit!

You are not an accident. You are a well thought out, pre-planned masterpiece that God as the artist has pursued through every moment of your life. I realize you may not be in a place where you see it. You may feel abandoned, or that everything about living as a masterpiece falls on you. You may feel lost in the storm all alone. Yet nothing could be further from the truth. God's light is piercing through the darkness and headed straight toward you. The picture given through Zechariah's prophecy at Jesus' birth reveals His ever-persistent, passionate pursuit of you: "Because of God's tender mercy, the morning light from heaven is about to break upon us, to give light to those who sit in darkness and in the shadow of death, and to guide us to the path of peace." (Luke 1:78-79) The path of peace is part of living as a masterpiece. The more you see and understand His pursuit of you, the more you will live in hope and, ultimately, a rich and satisfying life as His masterpiece. (John 10:10)

> **God has authenticated His work as His masterpiece by signing the canvas of your life before you ever existed.**

2. The *signature* touch

Most artists never sign a painting until they are confident they are finished with the piece, setting it aside as the very last thing they do. I have artist friends who have completed and sent a piece to a gallery, only to have the gallery owner send it back because the artist was so caught up in finishing the piece, he had forgotten to sign it. Yet the worth and value of any painting is based on the authenticity of the signature. When an artist has signed a piece, he's not only signifying that the painting is complete, but that the work has his stamp of approval. It's so important I will often prep the area on the painting where I plan to sign it before starting on anything else.

Life Palette

When I was in high school, I knew art would be a major part of my life, so I spent hours working on my signature. I wanted it to be unique and recognizable. I'll never forget the moment I arrived at the signature I've used my entire life. I was in study hall signing my name over and over with different nuances I had been working into the script. A friend asked what I was doing and offered a suggestion to the one part I still wasn't happy with. She was a godsend; it completed the signature that I'd been working on for several years. Since then, friends have tried to forge my signature. They get close but it's never quite right because they don't understand those nuances that make the signature unique.

God's signature on the masterpiece of your life cannot be duplicated. You're one of a kind and approved by His signature. But we assume that He, like most artists, signs the masterpiece after He is finished and when we stand before Him to hear the sweet words, "Well done, my good and faithful servant." (Matthew 25:23) Or perhaps we think God signs the masterpiece when we say, like Paul, "I have fought the good fight, I have finished the race, and I have remained faithful." (2 Timothy 4:7) Yet those words from Paul describe how effective you have been in creating your Life Palette, not whether He created you as His masterpiece. In reality, God has *already signed* the canvas of your life and declared you as His masterpiece. He sees the finished work already in the light of Jesus and all that He has done for you on the cross. The signature is already in place.

As an artist, I also sign a certificate of authenticity that's placed on the back of each of my original paintings, along with my personal seal, allowing collectors to know the work is genuine. In the same way, your value as God's masterpiece has been authenticated by His personal seal: "Now it is God who makes both us and you stand firm in Christ. He anointed us, set his seal of ownership on us, and put his Spirit in our hearts as a deposit, guaranteeing what is to come." (2 Corinthians 1:21-22 NIV) Paul adds elsewhere, "Having believed, you were marked in him with a seal, the promised Holy Spirit, who is a deposit guaranteeing our inheritance until the redemption of those who are God's possession." (Ephesians 1:13-14 NIV) If that's not enough to confirm you are created by Him and for Him as His masterpiece, He has written your name on the palms of His hands

(Isaiah 49:16). While it was a common practice to engrave a picture of something or someone you loved on your hands in those days long before photography, it also provides a beautiful illustration how you were sealed as His masterpiece by the nail-scarred hands of Jesus as He gave His life for you on the cross. The disciples saw this seal with their own eyes after the resurrection: "As he spoke, he showed them the wounds in his hands and his side. They were filled with joy when they saw the Lord!" (John 20:20)

Between the Palette Scrapings with Phil Starke

Without the artist's signature, a painting is just a painting versus being a masterpiece. The value is in the signature.

God has authenticated His work—your life—as His masterpiece by signing the canvas of your life before you ever existed. It is both awe-inspiring and impossible to comprehend, but it is nevertheless true and glorious!

3. The *framing* touch

There is nothing worse for an artist than to see their painting hanging in someone's home or in a gallery with a cheap frame that takes the piece in a direction far different than the artist intended. Edgar Degas is said to have taken one of his paintings down from a collector's walls with the intent of repossessing it because the original frame had been replaced. Artist Edouard Manet said, "Without the proper frame, the artist loses one hundred percent." One prominent American realist painter and printmaker is said to have written, "Do not remove this frame under any condition" on the backs of his paintings.

Why all the fuss about the frame? Because the artist understands the frame is the final finishing touch to their masterpiece. It doesn't just protect the work; it's a part of the work and enhances its beauty. A masterpiece does not look right in just any old frame. Try several different frames on a painting with a variety of wood stains or colors and you'll immediately see the difference. Imagine you were given a well-known masterpiece like the Mona Lisa and it was unframed. Regardless of how much money you had to spend, it's unlikely you'd just go to the nearest department store and purchase the cheapest, pre-made frame available. Since the Mona Lisa is a masterpiece, you'd either get the best frame you can find or, even better, consult an expert to help you make the right choice.

> **God's passion and signature is on the finished work of your life.**

Yet when it comes to the masterpiece of your life, how often do you take matters into your own hands? Framing is often an area you want to have control over instead of God the artist, but later wonder why your life is unattractive or doesn't seem right, causing you to blame God. It's sad, unfortunate and unnecessary. Your job is to focus on what's on your Life Palette, leaving the framing to the artist. The other problem with a cheap frame is it can cause such tension for the viewer that they perceive the art itself as junk. The right frame, though, will cause the piece to shine. Every brush stroke will come alive, and those who view the piece hanging on a wall will be drawn to it and it will speak the message the artist wanted to convey.

Of course, framing a painting is not cheap. Framing a masterpiece is even more expensive. Some people will spend as much on a frame as they do for the painting. Artists and collectors understand the value a quality frame adds to their collection. In 1991 at Sotheby's in London, one 400-year-old frame sold for $947,000. Eli Wilner, founder of a company in Manhattan that specializes in frames, says the finest frames "are works of art in their own right; they exhibit all of the qualities of any other three-dimensional object and some…are truly sculptures."

Others buy art from estate sales not for the picture, but for the value of the frame surrounding it. Perhaps the art had sentimental value for the previous owner and they invested in a valuable frame, or maybe they were a collector investing in an up-and-coming artist and hoped the value of the piece would increase so they framed it accordingly. Whatever the reason, they thought the art to be of such great worth they invested in a quality frame.

You, too, are worthy of a quality frame. Why? God's passion and signature is on the finished work of your life.

Love squared

You may know someone who has a painting or photo hanging in their home or office in a frame that's obviously the wrong size. My grandmother was like that. I remember an aerial picture of my grandparent's farm that hung in their dining room. The photo fit the frame horizontally but it was a few inches too small for the frame vertically. The result was there was about an inch of white space revealing the cardboard backing on both the top and bottom. I never asked grandma why she didn't frame it properly. Perhaps she chose the frame simply because it was just lying around the house, or she may have bought whatever frames were on sale at the time. It may have been that she knew it was the wrong size but so wanted to get the photo hung that she knowingly framed it incorrectly, intending on getting a proper frame later. Whatever the reason, it remained in the dining room, all off-kilter in the wrong-sized frame, until my grandparents went home to be with Jesus.

As the artist of your life, God has created the perfectly-sized frame for you as His masterpiece: **His love**. Anything other than that will simply not be the right fit. You may try to make other things work as your life frame—money, relationships, sex, some sort of substance, fame or popularity—but they never fit the masterpiece God has made. Why is it that all the self-centered passions we pursue end up looking like the frame my grandma used, with space below and above distracting the viewer from the picture as it was intended to be displayed? Simple: the dimensions are all wrong. We have been measured as His creation to fit perfectly in the frame of His love. Ephesians 3:18 says, "And may you have the power to understand, as all God's people should, how wide, how long, how high, and how deep his love is." His love is the perfect frame for the masterpiece He has created and, like any frame, it has four distinct sides.

The width of His love frames every experience you've ever had, and somehow uses it for your benefit and His will. "And we know that God causes everything to work together for the good of those who love God and are called according to his purpose for them." (Romans 8:28) It's not that He *caused* the bad or difficult things in your life; in fact, it's more likely that you allowed things on your Life Palette that needed to be scraped off and had no place being there. Yet God, in His wisdom and mercy, will frame it with His love.

The length of His love leaves no empty spaces and continues the length of your entire life and beyond into eternity. Scripture declares His love endures forever: Psalm 136 alone tells it 26 times. In Jeremiah 31:3, the Lord Himself says He loves His people with an everlasting, unfailing love.

The height of His love is perfect for you. In the most celebrated moments of your life, the highest highs, His love is framing you and paving the way for you to have the right relationship with Him, causing your life to reflect Him as a masterpiece.

The depth of His love reaches to your lowest moments, the darkest hours, those times of discouragement and despair when it seems that no one is there. Be it abuse, rejection, or when you did things you're most ashamed of, His love reaches down and frames those moments as a masterpiece. It's not that the consequences are removed or the pain is avoided; rather, His love covers it in forgiveness and restoration.

The Master and the Masterpiece

God is the master painter. Don't believe it? Spend a few moments and watch the sunset or the sunrise and you will see the splendor of the one who has painted your life as His masterpiece. In the Arizona desert where I now live, the sunsets are awe-inspiring. Every time I can't help but respond with, "Yeah, God!" as the colors are painted across the desert sky. Every sunset is a reminder of the quality of His work as an artist. All of nature is painted with His glory!

So are you! Take out your Life Palette and make it all it needs to be. The artist is waiting for you. As the Creator and artist of your life, God wants to display you for the entire world to see His incredible handiwork. When others look at your life, His desire is that they would see the masterpiece He created, framed by His grace and love.

Palette Points

1. How do you respond to the truth that God is passionately pursuing you because you are His masterpiece? What do you need to change in your thinking regarding this truth?

2. Take a moment and consider the incredible price God paid to sign your life as His masterpiece. What can you do to continually remember this?

3. Read Ephesians 3:18. Reflect on the width, length, height and depth of God's love for you as His masterpiece.

4. If you haven't done so already, memorize Ephesians 2:10. Personalize it. Live it! "For we [I AM] are God's masterpiece. He has created us [ME] anew in Christ Jesus, so we [I] can do the good things he planned for us [ME] long ago." (Ephesians 2:10)

My One Priority regarding the finishing touches:

Action Plan:

Meet Dr. Jeffrey Allen Love

Dr. Jeffrey Allen Love serves as the lead/teaching pastor of Alive Church in Tucson, AZ. With success at an early age as a painter, art has always been a big part of his life. While pursuing art and music in college, Jeff felt compelled to go into church ministry and has served faithfully for over 25 years. He has a B.S. in Theology and a Doctorate in Ministry from PHX University of Theology. His passion in life is to be all that God created Him to be and to help others be all that God wants them to be.

Jeff and wife Kathy have three girls and one boy. Jeff loves being a husband and father and centers many of his goals and desires around being successful in these two key areas of his life. As a couple, they have taught many seminars on successful marriage and raising children. Kathy spends her time focusing on selling Jeff's art work, allowing him time to paint, write, and lead his church.

Help others realize they are God's Masterpiece

If you found Life Palette helpful, why not share it with those you know and love. They will thank you and be glad you did! Help them get on the path of discovering and living their full potential. Here's how:

- Like and share my page Life Palette on Facebook: www.facebook.com/lifepalettebook

- Give Life Palette as a gift. Check out bulk prices on www.lifepalette.com

- Share the link for your friends to get a digital copy of Life Palette on www.lifepalette.com

- Share Life Palette with your pastor. Let him know that there are free resources available for every pastor and church at www.lifepalette.com including four sermon outlines for a Life Palette series, downloadable images for promoting a sermon series on Life Palette, and small group resources.

- Use Life Palette as a 12-week small group study. Use the Palette Points for discussion each week.

- Consider inviting Dr. Jeffrey Allen Love to speak at your church or event or with your leadership team. Available weekends are limited and are all prayerfully considered upon request. You can email Jeff at jeff@alivechurch.com

LIFE PALETTE

- Let us hear from you by posting your feedback on www.lifepalette.com on the My Life Palette Story page. Your story will encourage others on their journey to living life as the masterpiece God created them to be!

Pastors and Churches

Be sure to check out www.lifepalette.com for free resources!

- Sermon outlines from Jeff Love that you can adopt for your church to do a Life Palette series.

- Video sermon illustrations to use during a Life Palette sermon series.

- Downloadable small group material.

- Bulk discounts for books.

Consider inviting Dr. Jeffrey Allen Love to speak at your church or event or with your leadership team. Available weekends are limited and are all prayerfully considered upon request. You can email Jeff at jeff@alivechurch.com

Watch for

Lord Of The Fries

by Dr. Jeffrey Allen Love

Coming
Summer of 2014